Advance

Steve's book is a Bible study. It is not the casting of an opinion, a philosophy, or a political stance; it is a careful examination of the life of Jesus with the intent to follow. Anyone with a heart to follow Jesus will be interested, convicted, and inspired by this study. They will not feel judged or condemned, but they will feel challenged.

In this study, Steve unpacks the Scriptures in such a way as to answer many of the questions, fears and concerns Christians have about life, wealth and helping the poor. Questions like, Who should we help? Why should we help? How important is this? Is it a matter of salvation? What are we actually doing for the poor? These are important questions that many of us wrestle with. How we answer them says much about our religion and our relevancy.

Our world is dramatically changing. Today, nobody really cares what a man or woman's denominational background is, or their particular doctrinal stance about baptism. What the world looks at is what difference does our religion make? What impact does a person's religion have in their own community or in our global community? Is your faith relevant in today's world? If your church and all its members disappeared, would anybody notice? Jesus and his early disciples certainly made a difference. Their faith changed the world, and so can ours. Steve fans the flame of a first-century vision for the church that the twenty-first century church desperately needs. If we are to turn the world upside down as did our predecessors, we must show the world the full ministry of Jesus. The disciple earnestly striving to be like Jesus today will find this book deeply helpful and inspiring.

As one who grew up poor, I am grateful for someone like Steve being a voice for the impoverished.

—Robert Carrillo
CEO/President
HOPE *worldwide*

Dedicated to our grandsons:

Bradley Daniel Novack

and

Tyler John Novack

"Every good and perfect gift comes from above."
—James 1:17

JESUS AND THE POOR

G. STEVE KINNARD

Jesus and the Poor
Embracing the Healing Ministry of Jesus
© 2017 by G. Steve Kinnard and Illumination Publishers.

Printed in the United States of America. The cover design by Roy Appalsamy of Toronto, Ontario. Interior layout by Toney C. Mulhollan.

Illumination Publishers is committed to caring wisely for God's creation and uses recycled paper whenever possible.

ISBN 978-1-946800-69-5.

About the author: Dr. G. Steve Kinnard has served in the New York City Church of Christ as an evangelist and teacher for more than thirty years. He has preached and taught the Bible on every continent. He received his undergraduate degree at Freed-Hardeman College and his Master of Divinity with Languages degree from Southeastern Baptist Theological Seminary in Wake Forest. He then  completed his Doctor of Ministry degree from Drew University. Steve and his wife, Leigh, minister in Rockland County, New York. Steve also serves as Adjunct Professor of Bible at Lincoln Christian University and Professor of Biblical Studies at the Rocky Mountain School of Ministry and Theology in Denver. Read Steve's blog at "The King Jesus Herald," at https://stevekinnard.wordpress.com.

Illumination Publishers
www.ipibooks.com

Contents

Poverty
Written by a welfare mother in Tennessee[1]

You say you want to know what it's like to be poor?
Well, you've come to the right person. But you won't enjoy
my definition. ...
    I'm dirty, I'm smelly. And I have no proper underwear
beneath this rotting dress. I don't know about you, but the
stench of my teeth makes me half sick. They're decaying but
they'll never be fixed. That takes money. ...
    Poverty is getting up every morning from a dirty and
illness-stained mattress—a hard, lumpy mattress. Sheets?
They have long since been used for diapers, for there are
no real diapers here, either.
    That smell? That "other" smell? You know what it is—
that, plus sour milk and spoiled food. Sometimes it's mixed
with the stench of onions cooked too often. Onions are
cheap. ...
    Poverty is being tired—dog tired all the time. I can't
remember when I wasn't tired. When my last baby came,
they told me at the hospital that I had chronic anemia
caused by a poor diet, a bad case of worms, and the need
for a corrective operation. ...
    Poverty is dirt. You may say, in your clean clothes and
coming from your clean house, "Anybody can be clean."
Let me explain housekeeping with no money. For breakfast,
I give my children grits with no margarine, or cornbread

---

[1] When I was in seminary in the early 1980s, I took an independent study course for which I
read volumes of books on issues of social justice. I kept a diary of some of the best sections
of those readings. I entitled it *Devotional Readings for a Social Awakening*. As I started writing
the present book, I picked up my old diary and read through each entry. I've included
many of these devotional readings in this volume. Unfortunately, I don't have bibliographi-
cal information for every entry, but I'll give credit as I can. This first entry was anonymous.
"Poverty" was written by a welfare mother in Tennessee. It is quoted by C. E. Jackson in Stan
Mooneyham, *What Do You Say to a Hungry World?* in *Christian Herald*, January 1968.

made without eggs or oleo. For one thing, that kind of food doesn't use up many dishes. What dishes there are, I wash in cold water. No soap. Even the cheapest soap has to be saved for washing the old sheets I use for the baby's diapers.

Look at these cracked, red hands. Once I saved up for two months to buy a jar of Vaseline for my hands and for the baby's diaper rash. When I had the money and went to buy the Vaseline, the price had gone up two cents, and I didn't have another two cents. Every day I have to decide whether I can bear to put these cracked, sore hands into that cold water and strong soap. Why don't I use hot water? It takes money to get something with which to heat it. Hot water is a luxury. We don't have luxuries.

Poverty is asking for help. Have you ever had to swallow what pride you had left and ask for help, knowing your children will suffer more if you don't get it? ...

Poverty is looking into a future devoid of hope. Your children wouldn't play with my children; you wouldn't allow it. My boys will someday turn into boys who steal to get what they need. I can already see them behind prison bars. ... My daughter? She'll have a life just like mine, unless she's pretty enough to become a prostitute. I'd be smart to wish her dead already. ...

Poverty is an acid that eats into pride until pride is burned out. It is a chisel that chips at honor until honor is pulverized. You might do something if you were in my situation—for a week or a month. Would you do it year after year, getting nowhere, going nowhere? ... I did not come from another place, and I did not come from another time. I'm here now, and there are others like me all around you.

Introduction

I will never forget her face. I saw her in a parking lot outside a Hindu temple in Calcutta, India in the mid-80s. Calcutta was the poorest city on earth at that time. Her eyes were huge, like giant saucers in a sea of brown. Her pupils were dark, dark like the night. A sick yellow film filled the corners of her eyes. An English proverb says, "The eyes are the windows of the soul." When I looked into her eyes, her soul said to me, "I'm hungry, I'm starving, I'm desperate, I'm dying."

I don't know her age. I'm guessing she was between ten and twelve. Her hair was matted, uncombed, and caked with mud. Her skin was dark brown with a gray, ashen film over it. Her lips shrank back and exposed stained teeth under red gums.

She beat lightly on the car window. Then she put her palms together to form a cup. I wasn't sure what she said. I don't speak Bengali. I thought she was saying, "Please." Later I was informed that she was saying, "Uncle." I knew it was an entreaty. She was asking for a few rupees. She was asking me for what was equivalent to pennies in the US.

Her dress should have been white, but it was more tan than white. It had probably never been washed. It was so threadbare that when the sun hit it just right you could see through it to her ribs, ribs that protruded out of each side of her body like a keyboard on a piano. She was pencil thin. A swift wind would have swept her away.

She was one child in a sea of poverty. Dozens of children stood outside our car as we parked in front of the Hindu temple. They all had the same desperate look in their eyes. They all had their hands extended like bowls. They all pleaded, "Uncle. Uncle. Uncle." Charles Dickens would have identified them as street urchins. They were poor. They were helpless, hapless, and hopeless.

I was in my late twenties. I had lived a sheltered life in Tennessee, then North Carolina, then New York City. I had never seen the face of poverty—not up close and personal. This girl changed all that. Now I can't get her face of poverty out of my mind.

Her face. The face of desperation. The face of hopelessness. The face of despair. Her face.

What would have become of this girl if she had been born under different circumstances? Perhaps she would have been an educator, an engineer, a doctor, a social worker, or even an astronaut.

I rolled down the window and dropped some coins into her palms. Later someone told me that I ought not to have done that. They rebuked me for doing the only compassionate act I knew to do at the time. I was told that those few rupees would go to her master, her lord, her keeper, a man who managed beggars in that neighborhood. I was told that she couldn't keep those coins.

But I had to do *something*. What else could I do? I did the only thing I knew to do. I dropped a few coins in her palms hoping she would buy some bread or some rice. I was hoping that those few coins could buy her a few extra days on this earth.

I knew a little bit of money wouldn't fix her problems. I knew it was like putting a Band-Aid on a mortal wound, but I had to do something. So I gave her what she asked for.

Then we backed away from the temple and drove away.

But I've never forgotten her face. Over forty years later, I haven't forgotten. I don't even need to close my eyes to visualize her features. She is there in front of me as I type these words. I never learned her name. But I see her face—it is imprinted on my mind.

Her face was the face of poverty.

She was sickness, suffering, agony, hunger, disease, misery, desolation, anguish, gloom, and despair. She was helplessness and hopelessness.

She was one of tens of thousands.

Every day tens of thousands of people around our world die from sickness and disease that is treatable, preventable, or could be cured. Other tens of thousands go hungry and thirsty.

What is the Christian response to poverty? What is the Jesus response to poverty?

In the time it took you to read that last question, someone in the world died of hunger. That's right, someone dies of hunger around every three and one-half seconds. We cannot turn a deaf ear to the cries of the impoverished.

This book focuses on the ministry of Jesus, especially his ministry to the poor. Writing on this topic has proven to be a daunting task for me in two ways. First, when I write about the biblical response to poverty, I understand that I'm following the tradition of the prophets who gave a voice to the poor who had no voice. I am no prophet, but this message, by nature, is a prophetic message. Therefore, the task challenges me.

Second, I've never lived in poverty. I've never been poor. I've never been without adequate clothing or shelter. I've never been sick and did not have the ability to visit a doctor or buy medication for treatment.

I've never been without access to clean water. I've always had a roof over my head and a bed to sleep in.

I've never been hungry. I've simulated hunger by fasting, but being hungry from fasting is different than being hungry because you can't afford food or can't get your hands on any food. When I fasted, I knew that I could reach into my refrigerator and end my hunger. The poor don't have that luxury. They don't have refrigerators or cupboards filled with food. The poor spend the bulk of each day trying to find enough food to survive for that day.

This gives the prayer of Jesus—give me today my daily bread—new perspective.

My problem is quite the opposite problem. The poor have nothing. I have too much. I need to de-accumulate, to get rid of stuff.

My problem is not that I can't find enough calories to survive; my problem is that I consume too many calories.

My problem is not that I can't find clean water; my problem is that I've developed a taste for water filled with corn syrup and other sweeteners.

My problem is not that I can't afford medication, but that I might destroy my body from overmedication.

My problem is not that I can't afford clothes, but that I can't decide which clothes to wear.

My problem is not that I don't have shelter, but that I have too much house to take care of.

Yes, my problem is quite the opposite problem of the one the poor face.

Some might ask, "If you aren't poor and haven't experienced poverty, how can you speak about poverty?" That's a fair question. I've asked myself the same thing.

I'm not going to try to describe what it means to live in poverty. That's not my objective. My goal here is to communicate what Jesus says in the gospels regarding the poor and to describe the heart Jesus had when he interacted with the poor.

We claim to be a people of The Book. We claim to have no creed but the Bible. What does The Book say concerning Jesus and the poor? What did Jesus teach about the poor? How did Jesus respond to the poor? What is the Christian response to poverty?

The remainder of this introduction is taken from notes to a sermon I delivered on May 7, 2013 at the HOPE *worldwide* Summit just outside Washington, DC.

As I taught the lesson, I knew that I would be standing before people who were heroes to my wife, Leigh, and me. These were people who served the needs of the poor around the world, living out the healing ministry of Jesus. People like Randy and Jan Jordan, who at the time were leading HOPE *worldwide*. Bob and Pat Gempel, who started the HOPE*ww* work. Mark and Lin Ottenweller, who served the poor in Africa. And Gary Jacque, who led the HOPE*ww* work in Cambodia. There were many others who would be there also, too many to name.

I took the task of preaching on this topic seriously. I spent more time on this one lesson than any other single lesson in my life. I prayed about it, fasted over it, and wrote and rewrote it several times. Why did I take the lesson so seriously? I believe that when you speak concerning the poor in front of a first-world audience, that for that brief moment in time you become the voice of the poor, and the task of speaking for the poor must be taken seriously. I encourage you to take some time in prayer before you read too far in this book. Some of the material is hard hitting. I know it hit me hard. Jesus speaks about greed and materialism, and so much of first-world culture is built around greed. I wrote a chapter entitled "The Jesus Dream or the American Dream." I wrote another entitled "Bigger Barns." If you don't wish to be challenged by scriptures that speak against materialism, then close this book now. If you wish to be challenged, keep reading. But I encourage you to read and pray, and pray and read.

ﻋﻠﻰ ﻋﻠﻰ ﻋﻠﻰ

1 Peter 2:21 reads, "To this you were called, because Christ suffered for you, leaving you an example, that you should follow in his steps." This is a famous verse. This verse led to a bestselling book entitled, *In His Steps*, which led to an important question, "What would Jesus do?" which led to four initials, WWJD?

I grew up in a church that rarely discussed poverty. I went to a Christian college and majored in Bible. While there, I don't remember one professor discussing the Christian response to poverty. I don't remember sitting in one single class where the topic of Jesus and the poor was discussed. It wasn't until I went to seminary in the 80s that I began to understand that the ministry of Jesus was an integrated ministry that met the needs of the poor as well as ministered to their souls.

When I was in seminary, I read many books that made me want to be a missionary to the poor. I read everything I could find by and about Mother Teresa of Calcutta. She was a great influence on me. Her books led me to other books concerning Jesus and the poor. I was opening my eyes to a world I hadn't known existed.

One semester I took an independent study course with a professor, which I entitled "Readings for a Social Awakening." In this class, I read books that dealt with the Christian response to poverty. These readings planted in my heart a seed to minister to the poor. My wife embraced this same dream. We wanted to be missionaries in the Third World, specifically in India. The desire to be missionaries in India led us to the Crossroads Movement, which became the Discipling Movement, which became the International Church of Christ. We knew that if we were going to help people in India, we needed more training, so we moved to New York City to be trained so that we might go to India to work with the poor.

In the mid- to late 80s Leigh and I made three trips to India. On one of our trips, we met Mother Teresa (now Saint Teresa of Calcutta) in the airport in Calcutta. I spotted her in the ticket line in front of us. She was standing with four or five other Sisters of Charity, the society she began in Calcutta to take care of the needs of the poorest of the poor. The Sisters of Charity wear a white habit with blue trim on its edges. I spotted a small, frail figure dressed in a Sisters of Charity habit in the line in front of us. All I saw was her back, but I looked at Leigh and said, "That's Mother Teresa."

"No way," Leigh said.

"I'm sure it is," I replied. "But let me check."

I walked in front of the woman, turned my head in a nonchalant way in her direction, and almost jumped out of my skin. It was Mother Teresa. Here was a lady who had dedicated her life to the poor on the streets of Calcutta. I had read every word that she had written or had been published about her. I was ecstatic.

After we made it through the check-in line, I went to see where Mother Teresa was sitting. There she was, waiting for the same flight to Delhi that Leigh and I were taking.

I roused my courage and went up and started a conversation with her. We talked about a number of things. I'll always remember one thing she said.

I asked about the possibility of an American family adopting a child from India.

A priest who was sitting beside Mother Teresa overheard my question and said rather abruptly, "No way. That will never happen. The Indian government would never allow an American family to adopt a child from India."

Mother Teresa raised the crooked, shriveled index finger of her right hand and pointed toward the heavens. "If it is God's will, it will be done," she said.

That was one of the greatest moments of my life.

I saw Mother Teresa's luggage. It wasn't Gucci. It was cardboard boxes tied together with twine. When she won the Nobel Peace Prize, she bought two items with the money that accompanies the prize: a mop and pail. She gave the rest of the money to her charity.

While Leigh and I were in India, we also got to visit the house where Mohandas Gandhi stayed when he was in Delhi.

In the backyard there were clay footprints that led to a shelter where Gandhi would go in the afternoons to meditate. One afternoon, as he was walking to his place of meditation, a deranged man pulled out a gun, pulled the trigger, and took Gandhi's life. As you walk upon these clay footprints, you are walking in the steps of this great man. Being enamored by all things Indian, I had an eerie feeling walking in Gandhi's steps. I contemplated his willingness to die for a cause that he felt was important. I asked myself if I were willing to die for my beliefs. It's easy to answer such a question when it's theoretical.

Leigh and I never got to plant a church in India; we were asked to stay in New York. But as a consolation prize, we got to live in Jerusalem for a year. While we were there, I visited over fifty archaeological sites. The ones that always inspired me the most were the places where I knew Jesus had been, like the synagogue in Capernaum where he healed the demon-possessed man, the pool at Bethesda in Jerusalem where he healed the lame man, the steps of the southern temple mount where he walked to worship in the temple, and the Garden of Gethsemane where he prayed. I love the sites where we know Jesus was and we get to step where he stepped.

On Saturdays (Sabbath) our little church group would travel to the West Bank to minister to the sick and suffering in the Four Homes of Mercy in Bethany. We painted colorful murals on the walls of the hospital, sang songs, acted out plays, and fed the patients. It was thrilling to be engaged in the healing ministry of Jesus on the Sabbath in Bethany. Jesus had walked in this village. He visited with Mary, Martha, and Lazarus here. As we served the poor in Bethany, we were walking in the steps of Jesus and ministering where he ministered.

Yet I realize that you don't have to be in the Holy Land to walk in the steps of Jesus. I realize that I get to walk in his steps every single day of my life. Every time I decide to be moved by compassion to help those are hurting, I'm walking in the steps of Jesus.

Where do the steps of Jesus lead? They lead many places. They lead to a lost world that needs saving. They lead to young or weak Christians that need discipling. They lead to families that need strengthening. But there is one place where the steps of Jesus always lead—to the poor. Jesus stepped forward, stepped toward, and stepped up to meet the needs of the poor. He stepped toward the sick, the hungry, the naked, those in prison, the dispossessed, the blind, the deaf, the demonized, the leper, the alien, the stranger, and the immigrant.

Jesus stepped toward the poor because he had a compassionate heart. His heart showed us the heart of God. He was a living picture of who God is—a compassionate and loving Father. Jerry Shirley, a minister and author, tells this story:

> One day a little girl was drawing a picture, and even skipped recess because she was so focused upon it. Her teacher asked what she was doing and she said she was drawing a picture of God.

"Oh honey, you can't do that...no one knows what
God looks like," said the teacher.
The girl held up the picture and said, "They do now!"[2]

That's what Jesus does for us. He draws us a picture of what
God looks like—he shows us who God is. Jesus is filled with compassion. God is filled with compassion. Jesus loves the poor. God
loves the poor.

Jesus is the incarnation of God. He is God in the flesh.

My former professor, Rubel Shelly, suggests that the church
ought to be the second incarnation—the incarnation of Jesus to
the world. The church is the body of Christ, Jesus in the flesh.

When people looked at Jesus, they saw who God is. When
people look at the church, they ought to see who Jesus was and
who he is. As the moon reflects the light of the sun, the church
reflects the light of the Son of God.

Jesus ministered to the needs of people. If we are going to
follow in his steps, we must minister to the needs of people as well.
That's who Jesus was; therefore, it's who his people ought to be.

What is the Christian response to poverty? I have a deep conviction about this topic, a conviction that comes from Scripture. It
comes from reading the gospels and looking at the life and ministry of Jesus. I believe that we as a fellowship of disciples of Jesus
must do our best to meet the needs of the poor around the world.
I believe we need to teach and preach with more regularity on this
topic. I believe we need to integrate the healing ministry of Jesus
with the preaching and teaching ministry of Jesus. I think we must
constantly challenge ourselves in this area by looking at what the
Scriptures say about it. This is how we deepen convictions in our
churches—we look at the Bible. We are to be a people of The Book.

I believe that we as a movement have not been as urgent
lately to respond to the cries of the poor, the naked, the sick, the

---

[2] Jerry Shirley, "How Big Is Your God?" http://www.sermoncentral.com/sermons/how-big
-is-your-god-jerry-shirley-sermon-on-commandments-idols-124460.asp.

hungry, and the thirsty, as we were years ago. It saddens me to see denominational churches challenging their people in this area more than we challenge our people.

The cover story of the March 2013 issue of *Christianity Today* was entitled "The New Radicals." It highlighted several evangelical churches that were challenging their members to give up luxuries in their lives so that the poor around the world might have a little something. These new radicals were spending less on their church buildings so that they might send more money to help the poor.

If I want to hear a good sermon on responding to the needs of the poor, I don't look for that sermon on our ICOC websites. Instead I listen to David Platt, Francis Chan, or Scot McKnight. It saddens me to admit this, but it's true. At least it's true for me.

Thirty years ago that wasn't the case. Thirty years ago we were on the radical edge when it came to responding to the needs of the poor around the world. I think back to 1987 and the work that was done in the Central London church to awaken our consciences to the needs of the poor and destitute. Before that time, the needs of the poor were a forgotten or little-talked-about topic in our fellowship. Doug Arthur and Douglas Jacoby wrote a little book entitled, *I Was Hungry!* The Central London church made an appeal for our churches to get involved in meeting the needs of the poor around the world. I remember Doug Arthur, James Lloyd, Douglas Jacoby, and others preaching on this topic. I remember Mark Templer speaking about it. I remember sitting there in tears thinking about how much more I could do. I remember being challenged that there should not be even a hint of greed in my life. Those messages were prophetic. Those weren't "feel-good" sermons. They cut to the core. And we responded. We responded by opening our eyes to see the needs of the poor around us. We responded by opening our hands and serving the poor. We responded by opening our wallets and checkbooks to give to the poor. HOPE *worldwide* grew out of this appeal to help the poor. Bob and Pat Gempel organized this charity so that we could pool our resources and do more good working together than we could individually.

Over the past thirty years, God has worked through our churches to help the poor in amazing ways. But we can always take it higher. There is more to do. I haven't heard the biblical preaching on this topic in recent days like I used to hear it thirty years ago. For our convictions to stay fresh, we need to stay in the Word. We need to continue to be inspired by Jesus.

We claim to be a people of The Book. Our roots are in the Restoration Movement, which embraced the desire to restore New Testament Christianity. We claim that we desire to walk in the steps of Jesus.

And yet, I believe that if we are honest, we must admit that we are not as focused on meeting the needs of the poor and hungry as we were thirty years ago. The plight of the poor and what our response should be to their needs are not preached today from our pulpits as much today as they were then.

I am thinking about us as a movement of churches. I am aware that there are people in our movement who are just as committed or even more committed to helping the poor as any of our people have ever been. But, in my opinion, we as a movement of churches aren't as engaged in meeting the needs of the poor as we were. In my opinion, there are denominational churches more invested in restoring the ministry of Jesus to the poor than we are.

Back in 1987, as we began to plant churches in third-world countries, we became aware of the needs of the poor around the world. There was a great awakening in our souls concerning the ministry of Jesus to the poor. We were moved with compassion to to help the plight of people who could not help themselves.

I can't remember the last time I cried while listening to a preacher talk about the needs of the poor, the sick, the hurting, the lonely, the destitute, and the suffering. I can't remember the last time I felt convicted by a sermon on greed or materialism.

Thirty years ago, Doug Arthur and Douglas Jacoby wrote some challenging lines in their book *I Was Hungry!* On pages 42–44, they noted:

Listen to Ezekiel's plea to Judah (c. 590 BC) as he convicts them of their lack of concern for the poor:

Now this was the sin of your sister Sodom: She and her daughters were arrogant, overfed and unconcerned; they did not help the poor and needy (Ezek 16:49).

What was the sin of Sodom? Homosexuality—isn't that the first thing that comes to your mind? But that is not the primary charge against Sodom. Her sin: she was arrogant, self-willed, individualistic and aloof; she was overfed and unconcerned for the poor.

In our casual acquaintance with Old Testament history and our somewhat artificial ranking of virtues and vices, we usually consider homosexuality to be a far more serious sin than aloofness from the hardships of our fellow man. Both are bad, but look how we have excused ourselves!

We have in fact become a sister of Sodom—not by our sexual immorality, but by our attitude. It is tragic to realize that for many of us one of our greatest struggles is not to be "overfed." We struggle with our diet while the poor fight to keep fed. We struggle to keep up with fashion while they fight to keep warm. We struggle with our children's "higher education," while they fight to keep their children alive. In spite of these incredible inequalities, less than one Christian in fifty give consistently to the poor in any significant way. The more aware we are of the desperate need of our fellow man, and the less we do, the more accountable we become.

Though our consciences may be clear, had we been on trial with Sodom, accused of her crimes, by our actions and our inactivity the same verdict would have been returned to us: GUILTY!

Why is there a stubborn streak of "uncommitment" in some of our hearts that resents that verdict, and resists

> this message?... If you are growing uneasy at this point,
> **stop**. Search your heart, open your eyes—and your
> Bible—and pray for God to show you his will.[3]

At the time, these words were prophetic. They still are. Movements tend to be cyclical. What starts as a movement becomes a monument until someone (like God himself, for example) comes along to knock down the monument and get things moving. That's the history of God's people throughout the Bible. We speed up; then we slow down. We get excited; then we cool off. There comes a time when we need a revival. We need to be reminded of God's will and God's heart all over again. I believe that we need a revival in our ministry to the poor.

But you may say, "Steve, certainly we are in a better place in the way we serve the poor than we were thirty years ago." In some ways, we are in a much better place. I am continually inspired to hear all the great things that disciples are doing around the world to help the poor. We have disciples who want to help. We have funded and provided volunteers for many wonderful projects to help the poor: AIDS clinics in Africa, villages for people suffering from leprosy in India, a hospital in Cambodia, houses for earthquake victims in Haiti, and medical brigades around the world. HOPE *worldwide* is doing a fantastic job starting and overseeing sustainable projects to meet the needs of the poor all over the globe. We couldn't say this thirty years ago. We have made tremendous progress as a movement in meeting the needs of the poor.

Also, in most of our local congregations we collect a contribution for the poor. We have activities at least twice a year mobilizing our members to serve the community. Many of our churches have ongoing projects to help the poor. We have made great progress in our local ministries to be more engaged in meeting the needs of

---

[3] Douglas Arthur and Douglas Jacoby, *I Was Hungry, Second Edition* (London: Central London Church of Christ, 1987), 42–44.

people in our communities.

But, it seems to me, we have gone backward in our preaching and teaching from the Scriptures on this topic. The Scriptures give us a solid foundation on why we help the poor. Do we preach and teach on the biblical response to poverty as strongly as we once did? If not, our convictions are bound to waver.

Also, we should ask how many of our people are personally involved in helping the poor in their local ministry? It seems to me that the 80/20 principle applies here. Twenty percent of our people are doing eighty percent of the work.

We should also ask: How many of our people consider their gift to HOPE *worldwide* as equivalent to responding to the needs of the poor? Are we to equate our gift to HOPE*ww* as our compassionate act of service for the needy?

What are ways we can help the poor and needy outside of going to a HOPE*ww* event or giving to HOPE*ww*? Is there a local soup kitchen where we can volunteer? These types of local events are a great way to allow our light to shine to the world.

How much do greed and materialism mitigate the ability of our disciples to give more to the poor? Greed is like rust; it never sleeps. Greed is a constant barrage on the senses. A new iPhone is launched every two years. A new video game is released every few months. Clothes change with the season. Christmas shopping now starts before Halloween. The siren call of possessions, "Try me, buy me," rings in our ears. We must guard our hearts against the call of materialism.

These are questions I ask. These are thoughts I think.

You may disagree with me here. That's fair. We can have different opinions on this topic. But what we can't do is shy away from our responsibility to "proclaim ... the whole will of God" as Paul did in Acts 20:27.

Sometimes we need to be reminded of topics that we have left out of our preaching. Thirty years ago, we were prophetic in our call to restore the ministry of Jesus to the poor. Are we just as committed to that prophetic call today as we were thirty years ago? A sister in my ministry wrote me a letter a few years back. She asked, "Steve, why don't we speak about the needs of the poor in our church? I consistently hear sermons on evangelism, discipling, and family, but I rarely hear a sermon about our response to poverty." Initially, I was defensive. Then I started listening for it in our sermons (and in my sermons). The sister was right. I heard sermons on evangelism. I heard sermons about restoring discipling in our fellowship. I heard sermons addressing the needs of the youth and family ministry. But there wasn't much being said about responding to the needs of the poor.

At our conferences, how many speeches and classes are devoted to the topic of the Christian response to poverty? In your local ministry, how often is this topic studied? When was the last time you heard your preacher or teacher open the Bible and say, "Today we are going to look at what the Bible says about how we as disciples ought to respond to the needs of the poor." In our major seminars, HOPE *worldwide* is allowed to make a presentation. That is usually the ten to fifteen minutes we spend speaking about meeting the needs of the poor. Perhaps the plate is passed to respond to a particular cause.

Real, consistent preaching and teaching on this topic that was so central and vital to the life, ministry, and teaching of Jesus is seldom found in our fellowship. We need a revival!

When we look at the ministry of Jesus in the gospels, his ministry to the poor was who he was as a person. Jesus was filled with a compassion that compelled him in his healing ministry. He constantly spoke about meeting the needs of the poor and spoke against materialism and greed.

The aim of this book is to explore Jesus' teaching on poverty. As you read it, I encourage you to also read through the four gospels and make a mark each time Jesus mentions a poor person, speaks of the poor, or responds to the needs of the poor. I think you will be surprised at how much of the ministry of Jesus was focused on meeting these needs.

What can we do to renew our commitment to restore the ministry of Jesus to the poor? Perhaps we need to do what we did at first, or at least what we did thirty years ago. We need to get back into the Bible and let the Scriptures convict us in this area. We need to imitate Jesus in his life, ministry, and teaching concerning the poor. We need to renew our commitment to embrace and revive the preaching, teaching, healing ministry of Jesus in our churches.

ه‍ب ه‍ب ه‍ب

First-World Problems/Third-World Realities
GSK, 2017

I entered Panera Bread.
There was a line.
The cashiers were slow.
Slow as molasses.
I ordered a Bacon Turkey Bravo sandwich.
Audaciously, the clerk asked, "Whole or half?"
"Whole. Not half. And, could you put mayonnaise on it, not your special sauce, because your special sauce isn't that special?"
"To stay or go?"
"Go."

I sat in front of a sign that read,
Preparing ///// Ready.
Under the preparing side, came the name
Steve.
Then came the wait.
The wait for Steve to appear under Ready.
Eternity.
It seemed like eternity.
Tick-Tock. Tick-Tock.
Seconds passed like minutes.
My mouth salivated.

Waiting. Waiting.

Steve appeared under Ready.
I ran to the counter,
Grabbed the bag,
Reached for the sandwich,
Opened the wrapping,
Bypassed the pickle,
Bit into the sandwich.
No mayonnaise.
Not-so-special sauce.
Sandwich ruined.
First-world problems.

The child waited
For a crumb of moldy bread,
A taste of bitter milk,
A sip of rancid water,
A bite of dry rice.
She waited
And waited.
No crumb.
No milk.
No water.
No rice.
She closed her eyes.
Her mother called her name,
Cried her name,
Screamed her name.
Her eyes remained closed.
Her mother waited.
Eternity.
It seemed like eternity.
Tick-Tock. Tick-Tock.
Seconds passed like minutes.
The girl never got

Her crumb of moldy bread
Or taste of bitter milk
Or sip of rancid water
Or bite of dry rice.
Her eyes never opened.
Third-world realities.

Chapter One

The Life and Ministry of Jesus

In his ministry, Jesus reached out to everyone, to every portion of society in his day. However, when you take a deeper look at his ministry, you begin to see that proportionally he spent more time with the poor, the sick, the hurting, the helpless, and the hopeless than any other group within his world.

You might question, "Isn't that because proportionally the majority of people who lived in the world of Jesus were poor?" Yes, that's true. But Jesus could have selfishly avoided interacting with these people, like the priest and the Levite in the story of the Good Samaritan, who chose to step around the man who was beaten and left for dead on the Jericho Road. Instead, Jesus stepped toward the poor, the leper, the lame, the blind, the demonized, the hurting, the dying, the grieving, the hungry, the naked, the imprisoned, and the marginalized, and he taught his disciples to do the same.

What should our response be to the fact that we know the steps of Jesus lead to those who are in need? What does the Bible say is the Christian response to poverty?

Jim Wallis, the founder and editor of *Sojourners* magazine, found over 2,000 references to the poor, wealth and poverty, or social justice in the Bible. There is a Bible called *The Poverty and Justice Bible* that highlights these 2,000 references, demonstrating that there is almost one verse on this topic on every page of God's word.

Yes, you read that correctly. There is almost one verse concerning God's love and care for the poor and our response to the needs of the poor on every page of the Bible.

But it's not enough only to identify these verses. It's not enough to count the number of times the themes poverty, wealth, or justice appear in the Bible and conclude, "Wow, these themes sure appear often; therefore, they must be important." We are to be a people of The Book. We have to study these verses and see how they are presented in the text. We have to make sure that we interpret these passages correctly. We have to look at them in their full context and not rip them out of context. We have to make sure that we apply them accurately today.

A Crucial Passage: Matthew 4:12–25

You cannot separate Jesus' compassion toward the poor from his desire to save the lost. He loved the whole person. His ministry integrated care for the needs of people with saving their souls. He did both—as Jesus came seeking and saving the lost, he also gave sight to the blind, caused the lame to walk, enabled the deaf to hear, and cleansed lepers.

So let's ask: How did Jesus practice ministry? What did the ministry of Jesus look like? Jesus was the incarnation of *agape* love and compassion. He loved the lost; he also loved the poor, the hurting, and the sick.

Let's look at the beginning of the ministry of Jesus to get a picture of what his life and ministry were like. Consider Matthew 4:12–25. Verse 23 summarizes the ministry of Jesus. Matthew writes, "Jesus went throughout Galilee, teaching in their synagogues, preaching the good news of the kingdom, and healing every disease and sickness among the people." The ministry of Jesus had three facets—teaching, preaching, and healing. You can think of his ministry as a triangle whose three sides are preaching, teaching, and healing.

Teaching   Healing

Preaching

THE MINISTRY TRIANGLE OF JESUS

Side One: Preaching (What We Call Evangelism)

When Jesus heard that John had been put in prison, he returned to Galilee. Leaving Nazareth, he went and lived in Capernaum, which was by the lake in the area of Zebulun and Naphtali—to fulfill what was said through the prophet Isaiah:

"Land of Zebulun and land of Naphtali,
the way to the sea, along the Jordan,
Galilee of the Gentiles—
the people living in darkness
have seen a great light;
on those living in the land of the shadow of death
a light has dawned."

From that time on Jesus began to preach, "Repent, for the kingdom of heaven is near."

Matthew 4:12–17

Jesus came preaching. The word for "to preach" is κηρύσσειν (*karussein*), the infinite form of κηρύσσω (*karusso*). The word was commonly used in association with a herald who brought a message from the king to the masses. You've probably seen a scene in a movie like *Camelot, Robin Hood*, or perhaps *The Princess Bride* in which a king sends a proclamation throughout the land. A trumpet sounds, and the king's herald shouts, "Hear Ye! Hear Ye! His royal majesty, King ——, commands ..." The herald/preacher gives the royal pronouncement that everyone must hear.

What was the message of King Jesus? "Repent; change your hearts and lives, because the rule and reign of God has appeared." This proclamation was an important aspect of the ministry of Jesus. He came to proclaim to the world that the kingdom had arrived. As the King, he heralded his own proclamation that anyone who changed their heart and life and embraced the ethos of his kingdom could be a part of God's kingdom. The kingdom of God had arrived in the person and work of King Jesus, and Jesus proclaimed this message. In proclaiming it, Jesus came preaching. He came evangelizing, preaching the good news of the kingdom. Jesus came seeking and saving the lost. Preaching was one side of his ministry triangle.

Side Two: Teaching (What We Call Discipling)

As Jesus was walking beside the Sea of Galilee, he saw two brothers, Simon called Peter and his brother Andrew. They were casting a net into the lake, for they were fishermen. "Come, follow me," Jesus said, "and I will make you fishers of men." At once they left their nets and followed him.

Going on from there, he saw two other brothers, James son of Zebedee and his brother John. They were in a boat with their father Zebedee, preparing their nets. Jesus called them, and immediately they left the boat and their father and followed him.

Matthew 4:18–22

Jesus came teaching, which is different from preaching. Teaching implies research. It implies depth, and that the teacher thoroughly knows the subject. Teaching implies investing time to make sure the student understands the topic being taught.

Teaching brings the student to maturity. The task of making disciples begins with preaching the good news of the King, but it doesn't end there. After preaching comes teaching.

Jesus was the Master Teacher. He taught with his words and with his life. He invested his life in the lives of his disciples. They weren't easy to train, but Jesus kept after them until they understood what he was teaching. He never gave up on his disciples, and finally, after his death and resurrection, they embraced his mission.

Jesus taught the multitudes. He taught them through parables. People often define a parable as "an earthly story with a heavenly meaning." This is a trite definition that undersells the nature and purpose of Jesus' parables. Through the parables, Jesus revealed the mysteries of God's kingdom to an uneducated, unschooled audience. The parable was Jesus' way of communicating a rich, deep, spiritual topic to regular folk. It was his way of reaching the multitudes.

Jesus also came to teach and train a few. The bulk of the teaching ministry of Jesus was focused on those whom he called to be with him. He believed in training, in discipling. He trained his few disciples to carry on his mission after he was gone. Teaching was an essential aspect of the ministry of Jesus. Jesus came preaching and teaching.

Side Three: Healing (What We Call Benevolence)

Jesus went throughout Galilee, teaching in their synagogues, preaching the good news of the kingdom, and healing every disease and sickness among the people. News about him spread all over Syria, and people brought to him all who were ill with various diseases, those suffering severe pain, the demon-possessed, those having seizures, and the paralyzed, and he healed them. Large crowds from Galilee, the Decapolis, Jerusalem, Judea and the region across the Jordan followed him.

Matthew 4:23–25

Jesus took care of the whole person. In the words of Matthew, Jesus met the needs of "all who were ill with various diseases, those suffering severe pain, the demon-possessed, those having seizures, and the paralyzed." Jesus healed the hurts of people. That was who he was. He was compassionate and loving. He touched lepers, restored sight to the blind, caused the lame to walk, brought the sick back to health, freed the demon-possessed, and enabled the deaf to hear. Whole towns showed up at his doorstep. People came from miles and miles to experience his compassionate touch. The sick cried out when Jesus walked by to make sure they got his attention. Jesus is known as the Great Physician for a reason: he healed hurts. The third side of the ministry triangle of Jesus was healing, and it is on that side of his ministry that we are focusing in this book.

I've heard some change the "healing" ministry of Jesus to the "helping" ministry of Jesus. I don't think "helping" is a good substitute for "healing." "Healing" implies making a person well, making a person whole. In the Hebrew language, the word for greeting a person is *shalom*. The word means "wholeness." So when you greet a person with *shalom*, you bid the person to live in wholeness of life. The healing ministry of Jesus offers *shalom* wholeness to people.

There is a difference between helping a person out of a jam and healing a person. Healing implies that the person is made whole on the outside and the inside. In Mark 1, after Jesus cleansed a leper of leprosy, he sent the man to the priest to offer a cleansing sacrifice so that he could be accepted back into the community. He wanted the cleansed leper to embrace and to be welcomed back by his community. He bid the man obey the Law of Moses. Healing goes a step beyond helping. Jesus was concerned about the whole person, so he came to heal people, to make them whole.

Jesus went out "teaching, preaching, and healing," the three sides of the Jesus ministry triangle. In order to imitate the ministry of Jesus, we must make sure we include each side of this triangle today.

☙ ☙ ☙

If we are going to be a people of The Book, we need to embrace the whole ministry of Jesus, not just part of it. I've heard people say, "I'm afraid that if we focus too much on meeting the needs of the poor, we might take our eyes off evangelism and saving the lost." That's a real fear for some people. They are afraid that we will become a social gospel movement.

There was a movement in the late nineteenth and early twentieth centuries called the Social Gospel Movement. Its founder was Walter Rauschenbusch. Rauschenbusch is one of my heroes. I studied his works when I was in seminary. Like most of us, he was correct on some points and wrong on others.

Rauschenbusch and his followers believed that the first directive of the church was to improve the social condition of the poor. If the church did this, then this action would quicken the coming of the kingdom of God on earth. This teaching is called postmillennialism. The teaching went like this: if humanity improved the world enough, then Jesus would come. This movement died with WWII. After the war, religious scholars realized that if humanity were left on its own, the world would never improve. The only hope for the world was and is Jesus.

Rauschenbusch and other proponents of the social gospel had a liberal theological orientation. They didn't believe the Bible was inspired, that Jesus was born of a virgin, or that Jesus physically rose from the dead.

Our movement isn't like the Social Gospel Movement, and our leaders aren't like its leaders. We believe in the inspiration of the Bible. We believe in the Great Commission. We believe that Jesus died on the cross and literally rose from the dead. We believe that everyone needs to make Jesus Lord of their lives, repent of their sins, and be baptized to wash away their sins.

Just because a person believes in social justice and has compassion for the poor doesn't make that person a part of the Social Gospel Movement.

We can be benevolent toward the poor and remain motivated to seek and save the lost. These aren't mutually exclusive propositions. They fit together hand in glove. We can seek and save the lost and heal the wounds of people at the same time. How do I know we can? Because Jesus did. He is our model, and he calls us to walk in his steps.

I'm afraid that some of us think of ministry as something we "do," and we don't see ministry as "who we are."

Jesus didn't "do" love. He *was* love. Jesus didn't "do" compassion. He was compassion; he literally "suffered with" people. Serving others is not something we "do"; it's who we are as God's people. Evangelism isn't something we "do"; it's who we are. The gospel isn't something we "do"; it's who we are.

Embracing the healing ministry of Jesus will enhance our preaching and teaching ministries. A healthy focus on serving the needs of others will not take away from evangelism. Serving the poor strengthens our commitment to seek and save the lost. Why? Because when we serve, we embrace the loving, healing, caring ministry of Jesus.

I know some of us fear the social gospel. However, I ask, how can you walk in the steps of Jesus without the gospel being social? How can you seek and save the lost without having the compassion to take care of the needs of people? The gospel is social, but that doesn't make it the "Social Gospel." Let's not allow this fear to keep us from loving people and showing true compassion.

Our whole worldview is vastly different from that of the leaders of the Social Gospel Movement. Our whole theological orientation is different from theirs. I don't fear the Social Gospel Movement creeping into our churches. I fear greed and materialism crushing our churches. I fear us becoming a big, fat, greedy, materialistic, institutionalized denomination that has stopped practicing the compassion and love of Jesus because we are disconnected from the poor, the starving, the sick, the naked, the uneducated, and the dying hundreds of thousands of people on this planet that we step over, step away from, and step around each day instead of allowing our hearts to be moved by their situation and stepping up to help them. That's what I fear.

I fear the First-World dream that says we are entitled to enjoy our wealth while others fight to survive on nothing. I fear us getting so enamored with nice things that we lose sight of the millions and millions of people who have no things. Jesus never challenged us to fear helping the poor, but he did challenge us to beware and to be aware of the deceitfulness of wealth. We should fear materialism, the love of money, the deceitfulness of wealth, the hoarding up of possessions, and greed, which is idolatry. Helping the poor, seeing the faces of the poor, caring for the poor, will remind us of those materialistic evils that can destroy our hearts and cost us our souls.

The life and ministry of Jesus is described in Matthew 4 as a preaching, teaching, healing ministry. Jesus cared about the whole person. He came to seek and save the lost, and he came to give life to the full. Both of these aspects of his ministry were driven by his compassion for people who were hurting and helpless, like sheep without a shepherd. He became their shepherd, and ours.

The healing ministry of Jesus cannot be divorced from his preaching and teaching ministries. You can't have a two-sided triangle. If you take away the healing ministry, you no longer have the ministry of Jesus.

Let's look at our individual ministries and local ministries today. Let's make sure we embrace the whole ministry of Jesus. His ministry involved preaching, teaching, and healing. Do ours?

ﻋﻠﻰ ﻋﻠﻰ ﻋﻠﻰ

I Was Hungry[4]
Michael Quoist

I have eaten,
I have eaten too much,
I have eaten because others did,
Because I was invited,
Because I was in the world and the world would not have

---

[4] Michael Quoist, *Prayers* (New York: Avon Books, 1975), 78–80. I highly recommend this book; it's exceptional.

understood;
And each dish,
Each mouthful,
Each swallow was hard to get down.
I have eaten too much, Lord,
While at that moment, in my town, more than fifteen hundred persons queued up at the breadline.
While in her attic a woman ate what she had salvaged that morning from the garbage cans.
While urchins in their tenement divided some scraps from the old folks' home,
While ten, a hundred, a thousand unfortunates throughout the world at that very moment twisted in pain and died of hunger before their despairing families.

...I was hungry...

Lord, you are terrible!
It's you who queue up at the breadline,
It's you who eat the scraps of garbage,
It's you who are tortured by hunger and starve to death,
It's you who die alone in a corner at twenty-six,
While in another corner of the great hall of the world—with some members of our family—I eat, without being hungry, what is needed to save you.

...I was hungry...

Remind me of that, Lord, if I stop for a moment giving myself.
I'll never be through giving bread to my brothers, for there are too many of them.
There will always be some who won't have had their share.
I'll never be through fighting to get bread for all my brothers...

Lord, I'm no longer hungry,
Lord, I don't want to be hungry again.
Lord, I want to eat only what I need to live, to serve you
and to fight for my brothers.
For you are hungry, Lord,
You die of hunger, while I am surfeited.

Chapter Two

Who Are "the Poor?"

I knocked on the door. A big, burly man answered. "What do you want?" he barked.

I held out my empty grocery sack. "I'm collecting shoes for the poor in Africa."

"Why would you want to do that?" he asked.

"Because they're poor and don't have shoes," I said.

"Name one," he said.

"Excuse me?"

"Name one poor person in Africa who doesn't have shoes."

"I can't name one. I don't know their names. I only know that they're poor and need shoes. So my church is collecting shoes for the poor in Africa."

"Your church is doing this?" he asked.

"Yes, my church."

"That's not something your church ought to be doing," he said.

"Why not?" I asked.

"Paul said we need to do good to the family of believers, not to people halfway across the world from us."

"Actually, in Galatians 6:10 Paul said, 'Let us do good to all people, especially to those who belong to the family of believers.' And Africa is less than halfway around the world from us."

"You know there are poor people right here in Columbia, Tennessee that need shoes. We should take care of our own."

"Name one," I said.

He took a step back and closed the door.

I grew up in an ultraconservative part of the traditional Church of Christ in Middle Tennessee. I went to what is arguably the most conservative of the Church of Christ colleges. During my high school and college years, I never heard the topic of Jesus and the poor discussed.

Every now and then, I did hear a preacher quote Galatians 6:10. The preacher would use this scripture as a proof text to support his position that the church should take care of her own and not try to meet the needs of the poor outside the body. That's it. That is all I heard for the first twenty-two years of my life concerning Jesus and the poor.

Why do I mention this? Because some people still take this position today. They teach that disciples are only directed to take care of other disciples. They believe the church doesn't need to be concerned with the poor outside its membership.

I'm speaking of people within our own fellowship who believe this to be true. If these people weren't in our churches, I wouldn't feel a need to write on this. This is a real issue.

If the issue isn't real to you, then you might think to skip this chapter. But please don't. After all, I put my heart into it just like every other chapter of the book. It won't take much of your time. I use scriptures in the chapter and close with a nice devotional writing by Tamiko Yamamuro, so at least read the scriptures and the devotional piece.

ﻋﻠﯽ ﻋﻠﯽ ﻋﻠﯽ

When Jesus speaks of "the poor," who is he speaking of? Is he speaking of the poor in his Jewish community, or of the poor outside of Judaism? In other words, are we only to take care of the poor within the church or do we also have a moral imperative to meet the needs of the poor and hurting around the world? Is global poverty our concern as disciples? Or does the Bible only direct us to take care of the poor within the covenant community of Jesus?

These are important questions.

I believe that many of the verses that speak to taking care of the poor do apply primarily to taking care of people within the body. However, there are others that apply to a wider context.

It is important to note that when we compare scripture with scripture, we do see circles of responsibility that begin with immediate family and move outward toward all people. When we compare 1 Timothy 5:8 with Galatians 6:10, we learn that we are to provide for our immediate families and other relatives, and we are to do good to other believers and all people.

1 Timothy 5:8 reads, "Anyone who does not provide for their relatives, and especially for their own household, has denied the faith and is worse than an unbeliever." Notice the need to provide first for our immediate family and then our relatives. Compare this with Galatians 6:10: "Therefore, as we have opportunity, let us do good to all people, especially to those who belong to the family of believers." We are to especially do good to all believers, but we are also to do good to all people. You can see that the outward circles of responsibility expand from family, to relatives, to believers, to all people:

The Circles of Responsibility

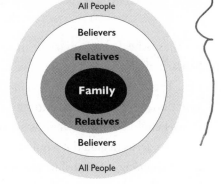

So the answer to the questions above is not "either/or" but "both/and."

We know that Jesus was sent only to the lost sheep of Israel (Matthew 15:21–28; Mark 7:24–27). Some argue that since Jesus was sent only to Israel, his healing ministry must have been limited to them. We also know that Jesus sent his twelve to the lost sheep of Israel (Matthew 10:5–6). Again, some would argue that the healing ministry of the twelve must therefore have been limited to Israel. The conclusion is drawn that if Jesus only ministered to those within his covenant community, we must limit our ministry to those within our covenant community (the church).

However, this line of reasoning is faulty because it overlooks two important points. First, Jesus met needs whenever and wherever they appeared, including Gentiles and Samaritans. We see this in several passages. Luke 17:11–19 reads:

> Now on his way to Jerusalem, Jesus traveled along the border between Samaria and Galilee. As he was going into a village, ten men who had leprosy met him. They stood at a distance and called out in a loud voice, "Jesus, Master, have pity on us!"
>
> When he saw them, he said, "Go, show yourselves to the priests." And as they went, they were cleansed.
>
> One of them, when he saw he was healed, came back, praising God in a loud voice. He threw himself at Jesus' feet and thanked him—and he was a Samaritan.

Jesus healed a Samaritan in this story. He didn't look at the Samaritan and say, "Hey, you. I've been sent to the lost sheep of Israel. Therefore, my compassion can't be extended to you and your situation. Sorry, you'll have to stay a leper. I wish there was something I could do, but my hands are tied."

No, Jesus healed the whole group. The one of the ten who was noted as being a Samaritan returned to thank him. (In all likelihood, all ten lepers were Samaritans, because Jesus was traveling along the border between Samaria and Galilee, but the text doesn't state that directly.)

At that time, Jews did not associate with Samaritans. The Samaritans had their own temple on Mount Gerizim in the ancient city of Shechem, the capital of Samaria. I should have typed "had" their own temple. The Jewish Hasmonean ruler John Hyrcanus destroyed the Samaritan temple in the second century BC. The

Samaritans continued to worship on the ruins of their temple during the time of Jesus. The act of desecrating and destroying the temple of the Samaritans demonstrates the hatred between the Jews and the Samarians.

Jesus broke social convention and healed a Samaritan of leprosy. He also had a conversation with a Samaritan woman in John 4 and invited her to drink water that would quench her spiritual thirst. Jesus made a Samaritan the hero of his parable that taught heartfelt compassion (The Good Samaritan). He crossed social barriers to minister to all people, meeting their needs regardless of their race or religion. He had compassion for all. He cared for all.

اللہ اللہ اللہ

In Matthew 15:21–28, a Canaanite woman approached Jesus and asked him to heal her daughter who was demonized. Jesus expressed to the woman that he was sent only to the lost sheep of Israel. But did the compassion of Jesus have a racial/ethnic/religious border that couldn't be crossed? Like any desperate mother, this mother didn't accept an apparent no for an answer. She pressed Jesus to give her only a crumb. He granted her request because of her faith.

There is the story in Matthew 8 of the Roman centurion who lived in Capernaum. Matthew 8:5–7 records, "When Jesus had entered Capernaum, a centurion came to him, asking for help. 'Lord,' he said, 'my servant lies at home paralyzed and in terrible suffering.' Jesus said to him, 'I will go and heal him.'"

Wait—isn't there a racial/ethnic/religious border that must not be crossed?

Jesus did not say, "I'm so sorry; I'm only here to help people in the covenant community. I'd like to help, but I'm afraid I can't. You'll have to find help elsewhere." He responded, "I'll come heal him."

Let's look again at Matthew 4:23–25. Matthew writes:

> Jesus went throughout Galilee, teaching in their synagogues, preaching the good news of the kingdom, and healing every disease and sickness among the people. News about him spread all over Syria, and people brought to him all who were ill with various diseases, those suffering severe pain, the demon-possessed, those having seizures, and the paralyzed, and he healed them. Large crowds from Galilee, the Decapolis, Jerusalem, Judea and the region across the Jordan followed him.

The news of Jesus spread all over Syria, a Gentile territory. Syria was, and still is, an enemy of Israel.

According to the text, people from all over Syria brought their sick, pain-filled, demon-possessed, epileptic, and paralyzed family members and friends to Jesus.

And he healed them.

He didn't send them away.

He didn't say, "Sorry, but my healing ministry is only for the lost sheep of Israel. My compassion doesn't extend to Syria."

Large crowds followed Jesus from the Decapolis and the region across the Jordan. These territories were predominately Gentile. The capital of the Decapolis, Scythopolis, drew its name from Scythian mercenaries who settled there. It was a thoroughly modern Roman city. It had a theatre that seated 10,000 people. The city contained Roman baths, a coliseum, paved roads, and all the luxuries the Roman Empire had to offer. Today an archaeological park sits on these ruins and you can visit Beit She'an, as the capital of the Decapolis is now known. It's an impressive site.

The large crowds that followed Jesus from the Decapolis and the region beyond the Jordan River would have been filled with Gentiles.

Yes, Jesus was sent to the lost sheep of Israel, but his compassion extended beyond Israel's borders. Jesus met needs wherever he went. His compassion extended to Jews, Gentiles, and Samaritans; it knew no territorial or ethnic boundaries. Jesus loved everyone.

Do any of us truly believe that the compassion of Jesus was limited to one racial, ethnic, or religious group? Do we believe the compassion of Jesus did not cross these boundaries?

We must be careful here. If we say the healing ministry of Jesus was limited only to the covenant community (Israel), then we aren't reading the Scriptures accurately.

رَلَى رَلَى رَلَى

Second (it took a little while to get to the second point, but we're here), at the end of Jesus' life, he gave his disciples the Great Commission that extended their ministry to the entire world (Matthew 28:18–20). The limited commission (go to the lost sheep of Israel) no longer applied to his disciples and does not apply to the church today. Therefore, the ministry of Jesus as he practiced it must be extended to the entire world.

This is undeniable. We know we must reach the world with the gospel of Jesus. We have developed plans to accomplish this goal. As we go, we also take the love and compassion of Jesus with us. As we go, we practice ministry as Jesus practiced it—preaching, teaching, *and* healing.

So, how did Jesus practice ministry? What did his ministry look like? Jesus was the incarnation of *agape* love and compassion. Jesus loved the lost, the poor, the hurting, and the sick. He extended his love to anyone and everyone. He had a heart for those who were separated from God. He also had a heart for the poor and destitute. Jesus loved the whole person; his ministry integrated care for the hurts of people with saving them from sin.

Any ministry that wishes to look like the ministry of Jesus must do the same today. Our compassion cannot be limited to those within the church. We must have compassion for all.

Night[5]

Tamiko Yamamuro

We prowl through midnight streets
Searching for homeless ones,
Thinking to find them shelter.
Here and there they lie,
Wrapped in torn matting
Made of rushes.

A garbage wagon
Is a bed for one;
Pillowed upon his arm,
He snores and snores.
There from a platform made of boards
A great, broad pair of feet
Stick out into the street.

Broken umbrellas,
Tied together,
Guard the man
Who mends them,
As he sleeps
Too restlessly.
His hollow cough
Follows us through the dark.
We pass a school;
Under the jutting eaves
Two children sleep
Upon the stones. ...

---

[5] Tamiko Yamamuro, "Night" in Toyohiko Kagawa, *Songs from the Land of Dawn* (New York: Friendship Press, 1956), 51–52. This poem speaks to me. I remember the first time I walked through the slums of Bombay in the late 80s. I thought of the ingenuity of the homeless to use whatever was at hand to make a home, a bed, and a boundary to guard their possessions.

Chapter Three

The Rich Man and Lazarus

In Luke 15 Jesus speaks about how we need to have compassion for the lost. He gives the parables of the lost sheep, the lost coin, and the lost son. I like to call this chapter the Lost Chapter. No other chapter convicts me more of the heart I need to have for the lost.

But Luke's gospel doesn't close with chapter 15. There is chapter 16 and the story of the rich man and Lazarus. Of all the gospels, Luke focuses more on Jesus and the poor than any other. If you want to do a quick study of Jesus and the poor in the gospels, study Luke.

Let's look at the parable in Luke 16:19–31.

"There was a rich man who was dressed in purple and fine linen and lived in luxury every day. At his gate was laid a beggar named Lazarus, covered with sores and longing to eat what fell from the rich man's table. Even the dogs came and licked his sores.

The time came when the beggar died and the angels carried him to Abraham's side. The rich man also died and was buried. In Hades, where he was in torment, he looked up and saw Abraham far away, with Lazarus by his side. So he called to him, "Father Abraham, have pity on me and send Lazarus to dip the tip of his finger in water and cool my tongue, because I am in agony in this fire."

But Abraham replied, "Son, remember that in your lifetime you received your good things, while Lazarus received bad things, but now he is comforted here and you are in agony. And besides all this, between us and you a great chasm has been set in place, so that those who want to go from here to you cannot, nor can anyone cross over from there to us."

He answered, "Then I beg you, father, send Lazarus to my family, for I have five brothers. Let him warn them, so that they will not also come to this place of torment."

Abraham replied, "They have Moses and the Prophets; let them listen to them."

"No, father Abraham," he said, "but if someone from the dead goes to them, they will repent."

He said to him, "If they do not listen to Moses and the Prophets, they will not be convinced even if someone rises from the dead."

What do we see here? A rich man who seems to have everything overlooks the needs of a man who has nothing. In the afterlife, their roles are reversed; the rich man suffers and the poor man is by the side of Abraham. One of the keys to interpreting a parable is to see where it surprises people. Most of the stories of Jesus contained a surprise. What's the "gotcha" or the "ah-ha" moment in the parable? The "gotcha" moment here is when the rich man dies and wakes up in hell, while the poor man is at Abraham's side.

For the first-century Jew, this was difficult to comprehend. Do you remember the conversation between Jesus and his disciples after the rich young ruler walked away from Jesus? The young man was sad because Jesus had commanded him to "go, sell your possessions and give to the poor" (Matthew 19:16–30; also found in Luke 18:18–30). Here's the conversation:

Then Jesus said to his disciples, "I tell you the truth, it is hard for a rich man to enter the kingdom of heaven. Again I tell you, it is easier for a camel to go through the eye of a needle than for a rich man to enter the kingdom of God."

When the disciples heard this, they were greatly

astonished and asked, "Who then can be saved?"

Jesus looked at them and said, "With man this is impossible, but with God all things are possible."

The disciples were "greatly astonished" at Jesus' comment concerning how difficult it was for the rich to enter heaven. They thought, "If the rich can't be saved, then who can be saved?" This was the mindset of many first-century Jews. They saw wealth as the equivalent of God's blessings; therefore, wealthy people must be saved. If the rich weren't going to be saved, then did anyone have a chance?

However, earthly wealth is not the equivalent of heavenly blessing. God expects those who are wealthy to use their wealth in a just and righteous manner. In the parable, the rich man was indifferent to the needs of the poor, and this went directly against the teaching of God on this matter. Therefore, God judged the rich man based on his indifference to the poor.

After all, the Old Testament is replete with references to the obligation of God's people to meet the needs of the poor. Consider these verses:

> There will always be poor people in the land. Therefore I command you to be openhanded toward your brothers and toward the poor and needy in your land.
>
> Deuteronomy 15:11

> The righteous care about justice for the poor,
> but the wicked have no such concern.
>
> Proverbs 29:7

> Do not withhold good from those who deserve it,
> when it is in your power to act.
> Do not say to your neighbor,
> "Come back later; I'll give it tomorrow"—
> when you now have it with you.
>
> Proverbs 3:27–28

The rich man saw Lazarus at his doorstep. He knew who Lazarus was and he knew his needs; he calls Lazarus by name in the afterlife, saying, "send Lazarus" to help me. The question to the rich man becomes, "Where were you when Lazarus was hurting?" Proverbs 21:13 speaks to this situation. I think it's one of the scariest verses in the Bible. It reads, "Whoever shuts their ears to the cry of the poor will also cry out and not be answered."

This is exactly what happened to the rich man when he woke up in torment.

Lazarus was laid at the rich man's door every day. It is possible that his friends might have laid him there. However, the poor are often enslaved to an owner or a manager who strategically places them around the city to beg. Perhaps this type of unsavory character put Lazarus at the rich man's gate.

Or this could be what scholars call the divine passive in the Greek. This type of verb implies that God initiates the action. If so, you could translate the verse as, "God laid a beggar named Lazarus" at the rich man's gate. Perhaps God put the beggar there as an opportunity for the rich man.

Lazarus was desperate. What did the rich man see when he looked at him? Lazarus was in pain, his body covered with sores. He couldn't afford medicine to ease the pain of his sores and promote their healing. Lazarus was so hungry he wanted to eat the crumbs from the rich man's table. He was tired, so tired that when the dogs came to lick his sores he didn't have the energy to beat them away. The dogs caused more pain. Imagine how it hurt when the dogs with their sandpaper tongues licked his open sores. When you read this story, you get a picture of desperation, helplessness, and suffering. That was the plight of Lazarus.

In contrast, you have the rich man. There he is, dressed in purple and feasting on fine food. In the first century, wealthy Jews grew long beards which they oiled with fragrant oils so they would glisten in the light. (Not unlike hipsters today). The oil for this rich man's beard could have been given to Lazarus to anoint his sores in order to promote healing. But the rich man overlooked Lazarus' pain.

When the man reclined to eat, crumbs fell into his beard and stuck in the oil. Old, stale pita bread was used as a napkin to scrap these bits of food from the rich man's beard. The rich man would discard the stale pita and the crumbs by throwing them under his table. He could have handed the crumbs to Lazarus, but he overlooked Lazarus' hunger.

The rich reclined to eat. This man's table would have been around eighteen inches above the floor. That's where poor Lazarus wanted to crawl to retrieve the crumbs from the rich man's meal. That's also where the dogs ate. The crumbs were left under the table for the dogs to lick off the floor. But the dogs weren't interested in the crumbs; they were more interested in licking Lazarus' sores. The rich man didn't care enough about the plight of Lazarus to call his dogs away from the poor man. He was that callous and indifferent to Lazarus' desperate situation.

What a sad image. Jesus was a master storyteller who could paint a picture with his stories. You see utter desperation on the part of Lazarus. This is what the rich man overlooked every day. You see coldhearted unconcern on his part. His lack of compassion toward the poor sealed his fate for eternity. In the first-century Jewish mind, the rich man had everything going for him. He should have ended up at the side of Abraham in Paradise. That is, except for the one detail that Jesus highlights in this story—he was unfeeling toward the poor. It would have cost the rich man nothing to meet the needs of Lazarus. Nothing except compassion.

What was the flaw of the rich man?

Greed.

Materialism.

Indifference.

Hardheartedness.

Lack of compassion.

James 4:17 states, "If anyone, then, knows the good they

ought to do and doesn't do it, it is sin for them." For the rich man, unresponsiveness to the needs of Lazarus was a salvation issue.

Who's to say that unresponsiveness to the needs of the poor is not just as much a salvation issue for all of us today?

One writer summarizes the story of the rich man and Lazarus in this way:

> From the scripture we learn that Lazarus lay powerless and helpless at the gate of the rich man. In fact, Lazarus lay at the precise location where every time the rich man left his home or returned, he would pass by him. But the rich man not only passed by Lazarus. He also passed him by. We can infer that in the rich man's eyes Lazarus became simply part of the landscape.
>
> The rich, indolent man had no concern for others. He got all he could and kept it all to himself. Every single day the rich man had the opportunity to minister to Lazarus. But he did not do anything to help the poor beggar. The rich man would not even give Lazarus the scraps from his table.
>
> So the rich man's sin was his indifference. He turned his back on every opportunity to become an instrument of God's grace to those in need. And in the end the rich man suffered the consequences of his daily indifference.[6]

I'm not sure where I first heard this quote, but I remember it goes, "Indifference or apathy is worse than hatred." I've also heard, "The opposite of love is not hate. It's indifference."

At least hatred is visible and can be pointed out to a person. However, indifference is like a cancer that spreads undetected until it overtakes the whole body to the point where it can't be treated.

Let's make sure we are sensitive to the cries of the poor. If not, our fate could be the same as that of the rich man.

---

[6] *The Fast That I Choose, A Biblical Study on Hunger* (Big Island, VA: Society of St. Andrew, 2009), 24.

I'll close this section with two practical points. They aren't original with me, so I'll quote them from their source—an article I found in *Themelios* by Hans Kvalbein. Kvalbein writes:

> We now can summarize the message of the story of the rich man and Lazarus in two sentences, a negative and a positive.
>
> 1. *A life of affluence and luxury closes your ears to the Word of God and your eyes to the need of your neighbor.* Wealth is dangerous for your spiritual life, for your relationship to God, and for your relationship to your fellow man.
>
> 2. Hear the Word of God and let it lead you to your neighbor in distress—while there is still time for it. The gate is open now. You can help your suffering neighbor now and care for him. Your action now has consequences for eternity.[7]

Let's look for ways to help our neighbors; and when we see opportunities to help, let's take advantage of those opportunities.

౬ ౬ ౬

Earthquake in Haiti, 2010
GSK, 2017

The plane flew into Port-au-Prince.
We got bumped to first class.
They served us hot chocolate chip cookies,
My daughter Chelsea and me.
We weren't prepared for the destruction.
Potholes the size of Texas,
Cracked asphalt,
Traffic at a standstill,

---

[7] Hans Kvalbein, "Jesus and the Poor: Two Texts and a Tentative Conclusion," in *Themelios: Volume 12, No. 3, April 1987*, 86 (United Kingdom: The Gospel Coalition, 1987).

Crumpled buildings,
Lack of infrastructure,
Political corruption,
Makeshift tents,
Shantytowns,
Children crying,
Families huddled around a fire,
A wrinkled woman snapping beans into a pot,
Traumatized, childless mothers watching.
No school,
No electricity,
No running water,
No toilets,
No bandages,
No antiseptics,
No antibiotics.
Open wounds,
Untreated sores.
Death.
Despair.
Destruction.
This was 2005.

In 2010 the earthquake hit.

Chapter Four

The Good Samaritan

A Good Neighbor[8]

by Dr. Martin Luther King, Jr.

Who is my neighbor? "I do not know his name," says Jesus in essence. "He is anyone toward whom you are neighborly. He is anyone who lies in need at life's roadside. He is neither Jew nor Gentile; he is neither Russian nor American; he is neither Negro nor white. He is a 'a certain man'—any needy man—on one of the numerous Jericho roads of life." So Jesus defines a neighbor, not in a theological definition, but in a life situation.

What constituted the goodness of the Good Samaritan? Why will he always be an inspiring paragon of neighborly virtue? It seems to me that this man's goodness may be described in one word: altruism. The good Samaritan was altruistic to the core. What is altruism? The dictionary defines altruism as "regard for, and devotion to, the interest of others." The Samaritan was good because he made concern for others the first law of his life.

Let's consider the Parable of the Good Samaritan, one of the greatest stories ever told. What can we learn about Jesus and the poor from this story?

Luke 10:25–37 reads:

> On one occasion an expert in the law stood up to test Jesus. "Teacher," he asked, "what must I do to inherit

---

[8] Martin Luther King, Jr., "On Being a Good Neighbor," sermon in *Strength to Love* (1963), 27.

eternal life?"

"What is written in the Law?" he replied. "How do you read it?"

He answered, "'Love the Lord your God with all your heart and with all your soul and with all your strength and with all your mind'; and, 'Love your neighbor as yourself.'"

"You have answered correctly," Jesus replied. "Do this and you will live."

But he wanted to justify himself, so he asked Jesus, "And who is my neighbor?"

In reply Jesus said: "A man was going down from Jerusalem to Jericho, when he was attacked by robbers. They stripped him of his clothes, beat him and went away, leaving him half dead. A priest happened to be going down the same road, and when he saw the man, he passed by on the other side. So too, a Levite, when he came to the place and saw him, passed by on the other side. But a Samaritan, as he traveled, came where the man was; and when he saw him, he took pity on him. He went to him and bandaged his wounds, pouring on oil and wine. Then he put the man on his own donkey, brought him to an inn and took care of him. The next day he took out two denarii and gave them to the innkeeper. 'Look after him,' he said, 'and when I return, I will reimburse you for any extra expense you may have.'

"Which of these three do you think was a neighbor to the man who fell into the hands of robbers?"

The expert in the law replied, "The one who had mercy on him."

Jesus told him, "Go and do likewise."

This is one of my favorite stories in the Bible. It has influenced the world so much that when you say someone is a "Good Samaritan" everyone knows what you mean. A Good Samaritan is a person who goes out of their way to help someone they don't know. Wouldn't it be great if the word "Christian" were held in such high esteem? "Christians" and "Good Samaritans" should be synonymous because both should mean "we love our neighbor as ourselves."

This story takes place on the Jericho Road leading from Jerusalem, which runs from 2,500 feet above sea level to the lowest point on earth—Jericho—which is 1,300 feet below sea level. The Old Jericho Road still exists today. If you are ever in the Holy Land, you should walk on it. It's majestic. It's not as dangerous as it was in the first century. I have several wonderful memories from my walks along it.

One of those memories is of the day Leigh and I took our children, Chelsea and Daniel, and another couple to ride along the Old Jericho Road. We had a devotional there, reenacting the story of the Good Samaritan. My kids wanted to be the robbers and not the Good Samaritan. Leigh and I should have known we were in for trouble at that point! Thanks to God's grace, they are both Good Samaritans today.

Before Jesus told the story of the Good Samaritan, an expert in the law asked him a question: "What must I do to inherit eternal life?" Lawyers typically asked rabbis this question. They also asked, "What is the greatest of all the laws?" They wanted to know the alignment of the rabbi—conservative or liberal.

During the time of Jesus, there were two influential rabbis who gave rulings on Torah law, Hillel and Shammai. One day, someone asked Rabbi Shammai, "What is the greatest of all the laws?"

Shammai didn't answer the question. Instead, he took off his sandal and started striking the poor questioner over the head, saying, "That's a stupid question. Never ask me that. Such a stupid question." The man got his answer and a few bruises. Rabbi Shammai was a conservative.

When Jesus was asked "What must I do to inherit eternal life?" he didn't take off a sandal and strike the lawyer. Neither did he directly answer the question. Instead, he answered a question with a question; in fact, with two questions: "What is written in the law?" and "How do you read it?"

The lawyer answered by quoting two commandments, saying, "'Love the Lord your God with all your heart and with all your soul and with all your strength and with all your mind'; and, 'Love your neighbor as yourself.'"

Jesus replied, "You have answered correctly; do this and you will live."

But the lawyer wasn't satisfied with this answer. He felt a need to justify himself, so he asked, "Okay, Jesus, but who is my neighbor?"

This sounds a bit like some people today who ask, "Now, who exactly are the poor? Are they the poor in the church or the poor outside it? Are they the desperate poor or the welfare poor?"

They are asking, "Who am I obligated to help?"

The lawyer asked, "Who is my neighbor? Who am I obligated to love?"

Jesus answered this question with The Parable of the Good Samaritan. To love your neighbor means to help those who are in need and to step outside national, religious, ethnic, social, and cultural borders to do so. To love your neighbor means to step up and meet the needs of whomever is hurting.

༄ ༄ ༄

In the parable, a man who was walking from Jerusalem to Jericho had been attacked by robbers, stripped of his clothes, beaten, and left to die. A priest came along and noticed him, but he passed by on the other side. A Levite did the same. They may well have justified their actions in the same way the lawyer attempted to justify himself when he asked Jesus the question, "Who is my neighbor?" If the man were dead, the priest and the Levite would have defiled themselves by touching a corpse. If the man was bleeding, they would become unclean by touching blood. So they passed by him without helping.

However, there is a law that overrides the laws of ritual purity. It's the law of love. It's the law of saving life. The priest and the Levite chose to ignore these weightier laws. Like the rich man was toward Lazarus, they were callous to the needs of the injured man. They stepped aside and stepped away from the man who was hurting. They didn't step in the steps of Jesus.

The "gotcha" moment of the story is when a Samaritan responds to the needs of the victim. Someone outside the covenant community demonstrated the love of Jesus, while those in the covenant community were hardhearted and callous. The priest and the Levite were familiar with the true fast of Isaiah 58, but they didn't practice it. Isaiah 58:6–7 reads:

> Is not this the kind of fasting I have chosen:
> to loose the chains of injustice
>   and untie the cords of the yoke,
> to set the oppressed free
>   and break every yoke?
> Is it not to share your food with the hungry
>   and to provide the poor wanderer with shelter—
> when you see the naked, to clothe them,
>   and not to turn away from your own flesh and blood?

The priest and the Levite literally turned away from their own flesh and blood. A Samaritan was the neighbor who loved.

At the end of the parable Jesus gives a directive: "Go and do likewise."

The priest, the Levite, and the Samaritan each had the capacity and means to help the injured man. Each had the opportunity to help. What was the difference between the religious leaders and the Samaritan? Heart and action.

On the one side we have hearts of callousness, apathy, coldness, and indifference. On the other, we have compassion, care, love, and concern.

On the one side is inaction: stepping back, stepping away, stepping over, and stepping around. On the other side is action: stepping toward, stepping forward, and stepping up. Stepping in the steps of Jesus.

Jesus extols the Good Samaritan and commands his disciples to imitate him—"Go and do likewise."

"Go and do likewise." That is the teaching of Jesus on meeting the needs of the needy: "Go and do."

Which will you be—the priest, the Levite, or the Good Samaritan?

Which will we be as a movement—the priest, the Levite, or the Good Samaritan?

Will we just walk by the poor, the needy, and the hurting? Or will we walk in the steps of Jesus, which lead to the sick, the blind, the crippled, the leprous, the demonized, and the poor?

Allow the words of Jesus at the conclusion of the Parable of the Good Samaritan to ring in your ears: "Go and do likewise." "Go and do likewise."

Yes, we must evangelize the world. Yes, we must strengthen, teach, and disciple our churches. Yet we must also minister to the needs of the poor. None of these directives of Jesus are optional.

We need not fear that if we give too much of our resources to help the poor, then we won't have enough to evangelize the world. Jesus, our model, did both.

The words of Jesus in Mark 10:25 scare me: "It is easier for a camel to go through the eye of a needle than for someone who is rich to enter the kingdom of God." Thankfully, Jesus went on to say that what is impossible with men is possible with God, but that first statement was designed to get us to examine our hearts.

There is always the potential to drift away from the teaching of Scripture. That's why we must constantly go back to the Word and make sure we are following God's directive. It's always a good practice to read and reread the Bible. It's always safe to take it back to Jesus.

What would Jesus do? Where do the steps of Jesus lead? As I get older, all I want to do is to learn more and more about Jesus. I want to sit at his feet and be taught by him. I love the gospels and spend most of my time in them. I want to be with Jesus, not just in the hereafter, but in the here and now.

So, who does Jesus say is our neighbor? Our neighbor is anyone who is in need. And whom does Jesus say we are to imitate in the story? The Good Samaritan. In this parable Jesus rang a bell that has continued to ring, ring, ring throughout the history of humanity:

"Go and do likewise."

ﺍﻟﻠﻪ ﺍﻟﻠﻪ ﺍﻟﻠﻪ

Abidjan, Côte d'Ivoire.
A HOPE *worldwide* Clinic. 1997 or 1998.
by GSK

Our host led my wife and me into a small cinder-block-framed building. Inside were several small rooms. Dim lights revealed green mold clinging to patches of tan paint on a plastered wall. Except for the mold, the walls were blank and bare. The rooms were dark, dank, and damp.

This was a HOPE *worldwide* clinic.

In one room, a fragile, thin Ivorian woman lay on a makeshift bed with a pillow under her head. I smiled and greeted her, "Bonjour."

She didn't reply. Why should she? I wasn't from Côte d'Ivoire. I was an intruder stepping into her world of pain and misery.

A nurse had strategically placed a needle in a small vein at the fold of her elbow. A tube ran from the needle to a bag perched on a silver pole.

A doctor from HOPE *worldwide* stood next to the woman.

"She's receiving fluid to stay hydrated," he said.

"What wrong with her?" I asked.

"She has HIV."

"What's the prognosis?" I asked.

He shook his head. "We are doing our best to keep her comfortable."

I understood what he meant.

The year was 1997 or 1998. I was from New York City. I knew what HIV was. Magic Johnson had made sure that everyone in the United States knew what it was. Magic was "magic," loved and adored. When he announced that he had HIV, everyone took notice. When I watched his announcement, I felt sad, and I prayed for him and his family. But I had never personally met anyone with HIV or AIDS. Now I stood face to face with an AIDS victim.

To my shame, I took a step back from the woman. AIDS was modern-day leprosy—a contagion which at that time had no known cure. Doctors were experimenting with drugs, and certain patients seemed to be improving from a mixture of medications. However, these drugs were expensive.

Leigh and I were escorted to another room. The doctor pointed to a shelf that held dozens of manila folders. I recognized them as patient folders.

"These folders," the doctor paused. "These folders are the patients who have died from AIDS."

My wife began to cry.

I was gobsmacked.

"If they had lived in the States," the doctor added, "they might have had a chance. The drugs for treatment are too costly in Africa. Here in Africa, HIV is a death sentence."

I'll never forget that long row of manila folders.

And that little word, "If."

Chapter Five

Bigger Barns

Let's take a look at a parable in Luke 12. This is the Parable of the Rich Fool, or, as I like to call it, the Parable of Bigger Barns. The parable is found in Luke 12:16–21, but to understand it better, we should consider the context, so let's read verses 13–34 to get the context.

> Someone in the crowd said to him, "Teacher, tell my brother to divide the inheritance with me."
>
> Jesus replied, "Man, who appointed me a judge or an arbiter between you?" Then he said to them, "Watch out! Be on your guard against all kinds of greed; life does not consist in an abundance of possessions."
>
> And he told them this parable: "The ground of a certain rich man yielded an abundant harvest. He thought to himself, 'What shall I do? I have no place to store my crops.'
>
> "Then he said, 'This is what I'll do. I will tear down my barns and build bigger ones, and there I will store my surplus grain. And I'll say to myself, "You have plenty of grain laid up for many years. Take life easy; eat, drink and be merry."'
>
> "But God said to him, 'You fool! This very night your life will be demanded from you. Then who will get what you have prepared for yourself?'
>
> "This is how it will be with whoever stores up things for themselves but is not rich toward God."
>
> Then Jesus said to his disciples: "Therefore I tell you, do not worry about your life, what you will eat; or about your body, what you will wear. For life is more than food, and the body more than clothes. Consider the ravens:

They do not sow or reap, they have no storeroom or barn; yet God feeds them. And how much more valuable you are than birds! Who of you by worrying can add a single hour to your life? Since you cannot do this very little thing, why do you worry about the rest?

"Consider how the wild flowers grow. They do not labor or spin. Yet I tell you, not even Solomon in all his splendor was dressed like one of these. If that is how God clothes the grass of the field, which is here today, and tomorrow is thrown into the fire, how much more will he clothe you—you of little faith! And do not set your heart on what you will eat or drink; do not worry about it. For the pagan world runs after all such things, and your Father knows that you need them. But seek his kingdom, and these things will be given to you as well.

"Do not be afraid, little flock, for your Father has been pleased to give you the kingdom. Sell your possessions and give to the poor. Provide purses for yourselves that will not wear out, a treasure in heaven that will never fail, where no thief comes near and no moth destroys. For where your treasure is, there your heart will be also."

You can see why I like to call this parable the Parable of Bigger Barns. It is the story of a man who has an amazing harvest, so big that his barns can't hold all the grain. So what does he do? He builds bigger ones.

His bigger barns represent greed.

In the United States of America, we live in a bigger-barn culture. Our lives are overflowing with stuff. We have so much stuff that we don't know what to do with all of it. Americans spend 22 billion dollars each year on storage units. It's difficult to get my head around the number *one* billion. Consider this: a billion minutes ago Jesus was alive. A billion is a very large number. In the US we spend 22 billion on bigger barns every year.

For many people, their bigger barn is a storage unit. Tom Vanderbilt writes:

According to the Self Storage Association, a trade group charged with monitoring such things, the country now possesses some 1.875 billion (almost 2 billion) square feet of personal storage. All this space is contained in nearly 40,000 facilities owned and operated by more than 2,000 entrepreneurs. ...

What this translates into ... is an industry that now exceeds the revenues of Hollywood (and doesn't have to deal with Tom Cruise). One in 11 American households, according to a recent survey, owns self-storage space—an increase of some 75 percent from 1995. Most operators of self-storage facilities report 90 percent occupancy, with average stints among its renters of 15 months. Last year alone [2004] saw a 24 percent spike in the number of self-storage units on the market.[9]

There is a television show called *Storage Wars* in which buyers bid on the stuff that people have left behind in their storage units. Viewers watch as these bidders poke their heads into a storage unit to see its contents. The bidders aren't allowed to touch or move anything. They bid on the storage units hoping that the renter of the unit has left something of value behind. The highest bidder wins, and that person (and the audience) gets to see what was left behind in a bigger barn. That's entertainment at its best. (My tongue is in my cheek as I write this.)

What can we learn from the Parable of the Bigger Barns? Two lessons:

1. Greed begins when you forget God.

The first verse in the parable sets up the story: "The ground of a certain rich man produced a good crop" (v. 16). Nothing wrong here. This is a farmer who had a bountiful harvest. That's what we

---

[9] Tom Vanderbilt, "Self-Storage Nation," *Slate*, July 18, 2005. In 2009, there were 46,000 units in the US, with more than 2.35 billion square feet of self-storage space, or a land area equivalent to three times Manhattan Island under roof. As of 2017, there are 49,000 units, according to the SSA.

would all like in life. It's okay to work hard and earn a living. It's okay to reap a bountiful harvest from our labor.

Then, as in all the parables, Jesus puts a twist in the story. Verse 17 reads, "He thought to himself, 'What shall I do? I have no place to store my crops.'" Here we see the first hint of what is going to be the Achilles heel of the man. He says, "I," "I," and "my." "*My* crops." This theme of "I" and "my" pervade the parable. In the Greek, it has fifty-one words; at least twelve are a first-person pronoun. There are eight "I's" and four "my's." I, me, and my are the holy trinity of greed. The man forgets who gave him the crops—where is God in all this?

The rich man makes the mistake of leaving God out of the picture. He acts as if crops grow without the Heavenly Father. Could the rich man produce rain? Could he call the sun to rise in the sky?

The problem is not the bountiful harvest; the problem is the man's perspective. Darrell Bock writes:

> He quite naturally wants to preserve his crops, but there is a hint of a problem in his perspective, for throughout these verses the major stylistic feature is the presence of the pronoun "my." ... The fruit of the land and other elements of the parable are repeatedly described with my: *my* fruit, *my* barn, *my* goods, *my* soul. Such language suggests exclusive self-interest.[10]

What Bock calls "exclusive self-interest" is also called selfishness or greed.

The rich fool forgets God. When we forget God, we've made a terrible, tragic mistake. We shouldn't ever be that forgetful.

When we get old, we do tend to get a bit forgetful—that's just part of getting old. I heard a story about three elderly sisters. Their

---

[10] Darrell L. Bock, *Luke* Volume 2: 9:51–24:53 in the Baker Exegetical Commentary on the New Testament Series (Grand Rapids, MI: Baker Books, 1996), 1151–1152.

ages were ninety-two, ninety-four, and ninety-six. These elderly siblings had never married and had lived together their entire long lives. As you can imagine, they were all getting a bit forgetful.

One night, the 96-year-old sister drew a bath for herself. She put one foot into the water, then paused and called out to her sisters asking, "Was I getting in the tub or out?" The 94-year-old yelled back, "I don't know, sister, but I'll come up and see." She started up the stairs, but stopped halfway and with a perplexed look on her face called out to her siblings, "Was I going up the stairs or coming down?" The "youngest" sister—the 92-year-old—was sitting at the kitchen having tea, and she listened to her sisters' interchange with a smirk on her face. She shook her head and said, "I sure hope I never get that forgetful," and knocked on wood for good measure. Then she yelled out, "I'll come up and help both of you as soon as I see who just knocked at the door."[11]

Age can make us forgetful, but so can possessions. The best way not to forget God is to make sure that you stay connected with him every day. Begin your day with a prayer of gratitude to God for giving you life and extending your life by at least one more day. Realize that every good item you enjoy in life comes from God.

Every now and then I walk around the apartment or house and look at "my" possessions and say, "This is a gift from God." Say that about your computer, your television set, your car, and everything else that God has loaned you. Don't forget God. When we forget God, greed attacks.

2. Greed makes us foolish.

The second lesson is that greed can turn a person into a fool. The story continues:

> Then he said, "This is what I'll do. I will tear down my barns and build bigger ones, and there I will store all my

---

[11] http://www.redlandbaptist.org/sermon/the-parable-of-the-rich-fool/.

grain and my goods. And I'll say to myself, "You have plenty of good things laid up for many years. Take life easy; eat, drink and be merry."

But God said to him, "You fool! This very night your life will be demanded from you. Then who will get what you have prepared for yourself?"

God said to the man, "You fool!" From all appearances, this man seemed to have it all. He seemed to be a smart businessman. He was making a profit from his farm. He had enough money to build bigger barns and store his grain.

But God called him a fool.

How does greed make us foolish? In at least three ways:

(1) Greed makes a person believe that life consists in the abundance of possessions.

Greed makes us believe that the person with the biggest and best toys wins. J. R. Miller writes:

> To look about, one would think a man's life *did* consist in the abundance of the things he possesses. Men think they become great in just proportion as they gather wealth. So it seems, too; for the world measures men by their bank-account. Yet there never was a more fatal error. A man is really measured by what he *is*, and not by what he *has*.[12]

Let me repeat that last line, "A man is really measured by what he *is*, and not by what he *has*."

Allow me to share a humorous story I read about a greedy man:

> A rich young man was driving his Rolls Royce on a mountain road when he lost control and his car went over

---

[12] J. R. Miller, quoted in William MacDonald, *Believer's Bible Commentary: Old and New Testaments* edited by Arthur Farstad (Nashville, TN: Thomas Nelson, 1997), 1418.

a cliff. The young man was thrown clear before the car went over, but his left arm was severed in the process. He stumbled to his feet, stood at the top of the cliff looking down at the burning wreck of his car, and cried out, "My Rolls! My Rolls!" The driver of another car stopped to help and heard him crying out like this. He gently grabbed the man and said, "Sir! You're in shock. Your arm has been severed! Let me help you." The young man looked down and when he saw that his arm was gone he cried out, "My Rolex! My Rolex!"[13]

Greed makes us equate quantity of possessions with quality of life. But God doesn't judge us by the quantity of our possessions; he looks at the quality of our hearts.

(2) Greed makes us believe that we are in control of our own destiny.

Greed makes us believe that we can choose how our lives are going to end. It makes us think that we can script what will happen in the future.

Look at the rich fool in the story:

Then he said, "This is what I'll do. I will tear down my barns and build bigger ones, and there I will store all my grain and my goods. And I'll say to myself, 'You have plenty of good things laid up for many years. Take life easy; eat, drink and be merry.'"

The rich fool thought, "I've got my retirement all planned out. I'll rest on what I've made. I'll kick back, put on a movie, order up a pizza, grab some sweet ice tea, and enjoy life."

This is exactly what many Americans dream their lives will look like when they hit retirement age. They want to kick back near a golf course so they can play eighteen holes in the early morning, take a swim in the afternoon, and play cards with their

---

[13] http://www.redlandbaptist.org/sermon/the-parable-of-the-rich-fool/.

friends into the night.

The problem is not the retirement fund. The problem is acting as if we are in control of our future. We act like we write the script of our lives. We act as if we are in control of time. That is how greed makes us dumb. We stash all this stuff away even though we have no control over whether we will ever get to enjoy it or not.

What are God's first words to the man? "You fool!" God's message for the man was, "You forgot about me. You were so busy getting rich and building bigger barns that you never considered that you might not live long enough to enjoy your success. You don't control how long you live your life. I control that."

Only God knows your future. He alone knows how much time you have left here on the earth. Only he knows what will happen to your possessions. Therefore, doesn't it make sense to think of God first in your life?

This rich fool made the mistake of thinking he had all the time in the world to kick back and enjoy his things. How foolish. We don't determine the number of days we live on this earth. Since only God determines that, we need to stay close to him.

(3) Greed makes us forget eternity; it makes us think that life in the here and now is all there is to life.

God said to the rich fool, "This very night your life will be demanded from you." The word for "life" (ψυχή, *psychē*) could just as easily be translated "soul," as it is in some Bible versions. So the text here could read, "This very night your soul will be taken from you." The man was so caught up in things, in possessions, in kicking back and enjoying the easy life, that he forgot that he had a soul. His life was all about life here on earth. He forgot about the hereafter.

God asked the rich fool a haunting question: "Then who will get what you have prepared for yourself?" Who's going to enjoy your things once you are gone?

You see, you can't take it with you when you go. Have you

ever noticed that a hearse doesn't have a trailer hitch? Have you ever seen a hearse pulling a U-Haul?

The ancient Egyptians believed you could take your possessions with you into the afterlife. That's why the pyramids were stocked full of gold, silver, rubies, boats, weapons, and grain. That's why they embalmed the Pharaohs. They even embalmed their family pets. They enclosed the servants of the Pharaoh inside the tombs while these servants were still alive, so that when the Pharaoh reached the afterlife, his servants would attend to his needs. This also guaranteed that the servants took good care of the Pharaoh during life. If you know that when the Pharaoh dies you are going to be locked inside the pyramid with him (or in one case, her), then you will do your best to keep the Pharaoh alive. But the Egyptians were wrong about the afterlife; you can't take it with you. The rich fool was wrong about the afterlife because he didn't even think about eternity.

Trent Butler writes:

> Riches have one major weakness. They have no purchasing power after death. They cannot buy the currency needed to get to heaven. Do not try to be rich in regard to the bank or barn. Be rich in relationship to God. Through prayer, study, obedience, and practice of the word, be sure you are part of the kingdom of God.[14]

Jesus closed the parable with this warning: "This is how it will be with anyone who stores up things for himself but is not rich toward God."

Jesus stated that the proper perspective for us to have is to think about how we can be rich toward God.

What does it mean to be rich toward God? Warren Wiersbe answers this by writing, "It means to acknowledge gratefully that

---

[14] Trent C. Butler, *Vol. 3: Luke* in Holman New Testament Commentary, edited by Max Anders (Nashville, TN: Broadman & Holman, 2000), 204.

[15] Warren W. Wiersbe, *New Testament Volume 1* (Luke 12:13–21) in The Bible Exposition Commentary (Wheaton, IL: Victor Books, 1996).

everything we have comes from God, and then make an effort to use what He gives us for the good of others and the glory of God."[15]

God allows us to have possessions so that we can use them for his glory. I heard a preacher say, "I have good news and bad news. The good news is that the church has all the money it needs. The bad news is that it is still in your wallets."

We should check our hearts. The problem isn't possessions; it's greed. We should ask: Do we love things too much? Is "enough" enough for us, or do we constantly want more? Do we enjoy giving to others? Are we selfish or selfless?

When was the last time you stopped yourself from purchasing something because you thought, "This money could go to a greater purpose than this purchase?"

When was the last time you sacrificed to the point that it hurt a bit?

When was the last time you drove a less expensive car, wore a less expensive jacket, spread out the visits for a manicure or pedicure and gave the difference you saved to the church or to the poor?

What do you hoard? Music, books, movies, technology, shoes, workout gear, jewelry, trips to Starbucks? What could you do without so that others might have a little something?

Let's not be the rich fool. Let's decide that we are going to be rich toward God.

علم علم علم

Scavenger Hunt[16]
Dorothy Day, 1970

A scavenger hunt is the latest game of "Society." A hilarious pastime, the *New York Times* society report calls it, and describes in two and one half columns the asinine

---

[16] Stanley Vishnewski, Dorothy Day: *Meditations* (Paramus, NJ: Paulist, 1970), 18.

procedure of several hundred society and literary figures, guests at a party at the Waldorf Astoria, surging forth on a chase through the highways and byways of Manhattan Island. "The scavengers' hunt of last night brought an enthusiastic response even from persons whose appetites for diversion are ordinarily jaded. The hunt was a search through the city streets for a ridiculously heterogeneous list of articles."

Any morning before and after Mass and straight through the day there is a "scavenger hunt" going on up and down 15th Street outside the windows of *The Catholic Worker* and through all the streets of the city. People going through garbage and ash cans to see what they can find in the way of a heterogeneous list of articles. The *Times* does not state what these things were but probably the list was made up of something delightfully and quaintly absurd such as old shoes, bits of string, cardboard packing boxes, wire, old furniture, clothing, and food.

If the several hundred guests at the Waldorf had to scavenge night after night and morning after morning, the hunt would not have had such an enthusiastic response.

Chapter Six

Was Jesus Poor?

A journalist with NorthJersey.com asked prosperity evangelist Joel Osteen if Jesus was poor. Osteen replied, "I never really thought about that."[17] If you are going to preach a prosperity gospel (that is, a message which teaches that if you follow Jesus he will make you rich) shouldn't you think about this question? If Jesus wasn't rich, why should we think his purpose for us in life is to acquire earthly riches? What do the gospels tell us regarding Jesus and his own wealth or poverty?

Some say that Jesus was wealthy. I've heard people say that when the Magi from the east visited the parents of Jesus, their gifts of gold, frankincense, and myrrh would have made Jesus a very wealthy baby. First, many scholars believe that these gifts would have been spent to fund the exile of Joseph, Mary, and Jesus in Egypt. They were a poor family from a poor village in Galilee who found themselves as immigrants in a foreign land. Second, when Jesus was dedicated at the temple, his parents sacrificed two turtledoves. This was the sacrifice of the poor, not the rich (Leviticus 12:2–8).

Jesus grew up in the small village of Nazareth. His father, Joseph, was a carpenter or a stonemason. Some say this would have placed Jesus in the middle class. The only problem with that analysis is that Nazareth had no middle class. Ninety percent of the nation of Israel at the time of Jesus was the *Am HaEretz*, the people of the land. These *Am HaEretz* were poor people who worked for and lived on a daily wage. Dr. Claude Mariottini notes:

---

[17] Jim Beckerman, "Celebrity Preacher Joel Osteen Comes to Northvale," *The Record*, http://www.northjersey.com/community/169993526_Celebrity_preacher_Joel_Osteen_comes_to_Northvale.html?c=y&page=1.

Jesus and his disciples were poor, according to archaeological evidence: Eric Meyers, a professor of archaeology at Duke University and editor of the *Oxford Encyclopedia of Archaeology in the Near East*, says he has personally excavated the village of Nazareth where Jesus lived. He pointed out that the Bible says Jesus was so poor that he couldn't afford his own tomb for his burial. "There is no way to speak of wealth in that context," he says. "This is living at the margins of society, eking out an agricultural existence."[18]

Jesus identified himself as part of the *Am HaEretz* in Matthew 8:20. He says he had no home of his own, no place to lay his head. Dr. Mariottini writes:

When a scribe came to Jesus and declared his intentions to follow him, Jesus said to that man: "Foxes have dens to live in, and birds have nests, but I, the Son of Man, have no home of my own, not even a place to lay my head" (Matthew 8:20). Jesus did not have a home to call his own. As an itinerant preacher he probably depended on people like Lazarus and his family and well-to-do admirers to provide for him and his disciples.

In Bethany, Jesus stayed with Lazarus and his family. In Capernaum, he stayed in the home of Peter. Jesus was a traveling rabbi who depended on the contributions of various people to support his ministry. Luke 8:1–3 reads:

---

[17] Jim Beckerman, "Celebrity Preacher Joel Osteen Comes to Northvale," *The Record*, http://www.northjersey.com/community/169993526_Celebrity_preacher_Joel_Osteen_comes_to_Northvale.html?c=y&page=1.

[18] Dr. Claude Mariottini, Professor of Old Testament at Northern Baptist Seminary, blog entry on October 25, 2006, http://doctor.claudemariottini.com/2006/10/was-jesus-rich-or-poor.html, quoting from *The Atlanta Journal-Constitution*.

> After this, Jesus traveled about from one town and village to another, proclaiming the good news of the kingdom of God. The Twelve were with him, and also some women who had been cured of evil spirits and diseases: Mary (called Magdalene) from whom seven demons had come out; Joanna the wife of Chuza, the manager of Herod's household; Susanna, and many others. These women were helping to support them out of their own means.

The gifts of the Magi were long gone by the time Jesus started his ministry. Now he depended on the goodwill of a few women who supported his cause.

To say that Jesus was a wealthy person is to misread the Bible. Jesus was poor. He knew how it felt to be homeless. He knew how it felt to sleep under the stars. He knew how it felt to depend on the goodwill of others for his next meal.

The word "compassion" means "to suffer with." Perhaps one reason Jesus had compassion for the poor was because he suffered with them.

Jesus certainly understood poverty. He grew up in an impoverished village in a region that was occupied by a foreign power. If we are honest, most of us must admit that we have no concept of how that feels. Yet a huge bulk of the world knows exactly how it feels. Jesus can relate to all those people much better than we can. The Apostle Paul spoke of the poverty of Jesus. 2 Corinthians 8:9 reads, "For you know the grace of our Lord Jesus Christ, that though he was rich, yet for your sake he became poor, so that you through his poverty might become rich." Paul speaks both in literal terms and spiritual terms in this verse. Literally, Jesus became poor our sakes. And through his literal poverty, we become spiritually rich.

My good friend Ryan McCullough gave me some feedback on this point. Ryan wrote:

Jesus was willing to be poor in order to relate to and help others, and we should be willing also (2 Corinthians 8:9). It really is remarkable that the God of the universe became not just a man, but a POOR man. How dare we think of ourselves as above adopting that attitude (and state) as well.[19]

The Poor

Close to half the world's population live on less than $2.50 a day.[20] That's less than a cup of Starbucks coffee. About 10% of the world's population live on less than $1.00 a day. According to the charity UNICEF, around 22,000 children die each day due to poverty. They die in small villages away from the media, so their deaths are anonymous deaths. Around 27 to 28 percent of the children in developing countries are underweight and underdeveloped. Out of the 2.2 billion children in the world, 1 billion of those children live in poverty. Every second child in our world lives in poverty. These statistics are staggering.

What should our response be? At the very least, we should have a compassionate heart.

Jesus was a Messiah who preached good news to the poor, freedom for prisoners, recovery of sight for the blind, and release from oppression. To be careful with our exegesis, we must say that you can take all these phrases to mean physical relief or spiritual relief. But when you look at the whole of the life and ministry of Jesus, you have to conclude that they mean both. His compassion extended to the physical and spiritual needs of people.

I've often heard people say that Jesus' mission statement was Luke 19:10, "For the Son of Man came to seek and to save what was lost." Or they say it was Matthew 28:18–20, the Great Commission.

---

[19] Personal correspondence on August 11, 2017.

[20] http://www.globalissues.org/article/26/poverty-facts-and-stats.

It's not best to truncate the purpose of Jesus' ministry down to one verse in the gospels. In the gospels, Jesus gave at least ten "I have come" statements. They are:

1. **Mark 1:38.** I have come to preach.
2. **Mark 2:17; Luke 5:32.** I have come to call sinners.
3. **Mark 10:45; Matthew 20:28.** I have come to serve.
4. **Mark 10:45; Matthew 20:28.** I have come to give my life as a ransom.
5. **John 6:38–39.** I have come to do God's will (i.e., to keep the saved, saved).
6. **John 9:39.** I have come for judgment.
7. **John 10:10.** I have come to give abundant life.
8. **John 12:46.** I have come to be a light to lead people to God.
9. **John 12:47.** I have come not to judge the world, but to save it.
10. **John 18:37.** I have come to testify to the truth.

Jesus came to seek and save the lost, but he also came to serve. Jesus came to save the world, but he also came so that people might have abundant life. We need to get a fuller picture of the purpose and mission of Jesus throughout his life and ministry.

Jesus did everything well. People noticed this about him in connection with his healing ministry. Mark 7:37 states, "People were overwhelmed with amazement. 'He has done everything well,' they said. 'He even makes the deaf hear and the mute speak.'" Jesus did everything well; he could seek and save the lost while meeting the physical needs of people.

Jesus was compassionate. He didn't step around people when they were hurting. In the story of the rich man and Lazarus, the rich man stepped around Lazarus. And the rich man's final destiny was "hell, where he was in torment" (Luke 16:23).

Jesus didn't step around the poor; he stepped up and met their needs. He didn't step around suffering people; he stepped toward the suffering and met needs. If we are going to walk in the steps of Jesus, our steps will follow him there. One time, an entire village brought their sick and demon-possessed to Jesus. He didn't step away. He stepped up and healed many (Mark 1:29–34). We can't step around, step over, step away from the poor. We need to step up and step toward the poor and suffering and do our best to meet their needs.

When John the Baptist was in prison, he sent his disciples to ask Jesus if he was the Messiah. Jesus sent the disciples back to John with a message.

The message didn't say, "Tell John how many people were baptized today."

The message didn't say, "Tell John how many people I got with and discipled today."

The message was:

> "Go back and report to John what you have seen and heard: The blind receive sight, the lame walk, those who have leprosy are cured, the deaf hear, the dead are raised, and the good news is preached to the poor. Blessed is the man who does not fall away on account of me."
>
> Luke 7:22

That's not to say that Jesus was not seeking and saving the lost. He was. However, we cannot divorce the healing ministry of Jesus from his preaching ministry. They are two sides of the same coin. The coin is the compassion of Jesus.

We must be people who, like Jesus, are filled with and moved by compassion.

Compassion for the lost.

Compassion for the poor and needy.

Compassion for those who are unlike us.

Compassion for those who suffer from mental illness.

Compassion for the old and aged.

Compassion for immigrants.

If we lose our heart for people, are we still walking in the steps of Jesus?

If every evangelist in our movement of churches were to preach through books of the Bible on Sundays and at midweek services, this would multiply the number of lessons we hear each year on God's love for the poor and helpless. Imagine trying to teach the epistle of James or the gospel of Luke or 1 Corinthians without mentioning God's compassion and love for the poor and suffering.

If we overtly or covertly teach that we can reach the world for Jesus without having a heart for the poor, we have misread a huge portion of the gospels. Do we preach on Luke 15 and omit Luke 16? Do we preach Matthew 28:18–20 and leave out Matthew 4:23–24?

Will disciples in our churches grow and mature as they ought without a proper emphasis on loving our neighbors as Jesus defined what it means to do so? Will our disciples grow if they are left unchallenged concerning greed or materialism? Perhaps we are afraid that if we challenge disciples concerning their greedy hearts, they might very well challenge us back!

What would we say to Joe Christian who says, "I give to missions, therefore I'm evangelistic"?

Or what might we say to Sally Christian who says, "I contribute to the evangelist's salary, therefore I am discipling others"?

Yet we seem content to allow Joe or Sally Christian to think that their contribution to a charity is the equivalent of meeting the needs of the poor.

Do we take care of the beggar at our own gate?

After all, that beggar in the first century might have been

Jesus. Jesus wasn't part of the landed gentry. He wasn't a high priest who lived in luxury in Jerusalem. Jesus was the son of a carpenter from a backwater village in Galilee who taught people to pray for their daily bread because he knew what it was like to be a day laborer who lived on his daily wage.

Jesus could relate to the poor because he knew what it was like to be poor.

عَلَمَ عَلَمَ عَلَمَ

Medical Care
by GSK, 2017

In the States, we tend to complain about medical insurance. The premiums continue to rise. The co-pays get higher and higher. There are more and more forms to fill out. Often these forms seem to be written in code.

A mother felt soreness in her chest cavity. The pain was on the left side. She figured it was a pulled muscle.

During a visit to her gynecologist, she mentioned the chest pain.

"You have to get to a cardiologist immediately," her doctor said. "You can't self-diagnose a pain in your chest."

Message received.

Within thirty minutes, the mother was speaking with a cardiologist.

The cardiologist gave her an echocardiogram. He performed a stress test on her.

The results were inconclusive.

So he ordered a blood test, a CAT scan on the chest, and a more extensive echo.

The soreness could have been a pulled muscle.

It could have come from picking up her daughter.

It could have come from wresting with her son's.

On the other side of the world, a mother picks up her daughter. She feels pain in her chest. The pain is on the left side of her chest.

What is causing the pain?

She'll never know for sure. She'll either live with the pain or die from whatever is causing it.

There are no insurance premiums, no co-pays, no lengthy, indecipherable forms to fill out.

When you don't have doctors, hospitals, clinics, or medical labs, there is no need for insurance.

What you are left with is pain.

Pain, then death.

Chapter Seven

Jesus with the Poor

I remember reading a story of a married woman who kept a box under her bed. She didn't hide the box from her husband, but she did ask her husband not to look in it.

Finally, after years of being tempted to look in the box, the husband gave in to the temptation and looked.

He was surprised to find two chicken eggs and a stack of one-hundred-dollar bills. He confessed to his wife that he had looked in the box. "What's the deal with the chicken eggs?" he asked.

"Early in our marriage," said the wife, "I knew that I was being too judgmental and critical of you, so every time I felt like you had blown it, I put a chicken egg in the box."

Her husband was taken aback. "I know you love me and respect me," he said, "but I've messed up a lot more than two times over the years. By the way, where did the huge stack of hundreds come from?"

"Every time I collected a dozen eggs," the woman replied, "I sold them."

We are all sinners who have made mistake after mistake. One area where we sometimes make mistakes is in the area of helping the poor.

Why have a heart for the poor? Because Jesus did. Jesus had compassion on those who were less fortunate than others. He had a compassionate heart for those who were stricken with disease and sickness. He healed the sick, made the lame walk, cleansed lepers, gave new life to the demonized, and caused the blind to see and the deaf to hear.

Here are some verses in the gospels that describe Jesus' ministry to the poor.

> Jesus went through all the towns and villages, teaching in their synagogues, preaching the good news of the kingdom and healing every disease and sickness. When he saw the crowds, he had compassion on them, because they were harassed and helpless, like sheep without a shepherd. Then he said to his disciples, "The harvest is plentiful but the workers are few."
>
> Matthew 9:35–37

Every coin has two sides. The two sides to the coin of compassion in the ministry of Jesus are preaching and healing.

> Jesus replied, "'Love the Lord your God with all your heart and with all your soul and with all your mind.' This is the first and greatest commandment. And the second is like it: 'Love your neighbor as yourself.' All the Law and the Prophets hang on these two commandments."
>
> Matthew 22:37–40

Jesus said, "Love your neighbor." Then, in the Parable of the Good Samaritan, he defined your neighbor as anyone who has needs. When we love our neighbor, we meet the needs of other people.

> When Jesus heard what had happened, he withdrew by boat privately to a solitary place. Hearing of this, the crowds followed him on foot from the towns. When Jesus landed and saw a large crowd, he had compassion on them and healed their sick.
>
> Matthew 14:13–14

Notice that the compassion of Jesus leads to healing the sick.

As Jesus and his disciples were leaving Jericho, a large crowd followed him. Two blind men were sitting by the roadside, and when they heard that Jesus was going by, they shouted, "Lord, Son of David, have mercy on us!"

The crowd rebuked them and told them to be quiet, but they shouted all the louder, "Lord, Son of David, have mercy on us!"

Jesus stopped and called them. "What do you want me to do for you?" he asked.

"Lord," they answered, "we want our sight."

Jesus had compassion on them and touched their eyes. Immediately they received their sight and followed him.

Matthew 20:29–34

This is a tender story. It is set in Jericho, which sits in the bottom of the Great Syrian-African Rift Valley some 1,300 feet below sea level. Jericho and Damascus bid for the title of being the oldest continually occupied city in the world. I love Jericho. I've eaten many a great Arab dinner there. In the first century, Jericho was rife with poverty, and poverty continues to plague the city today.

As Jesus was leaving the city, two blind men heard that he was passing their way. They began to shout out, "Lord, Son of David, have mercy on us!" The blind men used a messianic title, Son of David, to refer to Jesus. They called him "Lord," which means "master." They asked for mercy. The Hebrew word for mercy is *hesed*. God is the giver of *hesed*. These two blind men understood that Jesus was Messiah, Lord, and God. These two blind men saw Jesus more clearly than his own disciples saw him; though they were blind, they had 20/20 spiritual vision.

The crowd that followed Jesus rebuked the two blind men and told them to stop shouting. Instead, the men shouted even louder, "Lord, Son of David, have mercy on us!"

Jesus stopped.

He called them.

Jesus asked, "What can I do for you?"

"We want our sight," said the blind men.

Jesus was moved with compassion, and when Jesus was moved by compassion, he healed people. That was his ministry.

After receiving their sight, the two men followed Jesus. They became his disciples. And where was Jesus leading them? He was taking them up to Jerusalem. And what happened to Jesus in Jerusalem? He was crucified. The unblinded men followed Jesus to his death. That's always the path of discipleship. When we decide to follow Jesus, he leads us to a cross.

> A man with leprosy came to him and begged him on his knees, "If you are willing, you can make me clean."
>
> Jesus was indignant. He reached out his hand and touched the man. "I am willing," he said. "Be clean!" Immediately the leprosy left him and he was cleansed.
>
> Jesus sent him away at once with a strong warning: "See that you don't tell this to anyone. But go, show yourself to the priest and offer the sacrifices that Moses commanded for your cleansing, as a testimony to them." Instead he went out and began to talk freely, spreading the news. As a result, Jesus could no longer enter a town openly but stayed outside in lonely places. Yet the people still came to him from everywhere.
>
> Mark 1:40–45

A leper threw himself at the feet of Jesus and begged to be healed. Jesus reached out his hand, touched the leper, and healed him.

Why? Some ancient manuscripts say, "Jesus was indignant." He wasn't indignant with the man, but at the disease that caused the man to suffer for so many years. Other Greek manuscripts read, "Jesus was filled with compassion."

The English word "compassion" comes from two Greeks words, *cum* and *pathos,* which mean "with," and "suffer," respectively.

When you have compassion for someone, you suffer with that person.

In the Hebrew, the word for compassion is the plural form of a word, which in the singular means "womb." Thus, the feeling of compassion is associated with the womb of a woman and with the stomach, bowels, or loins of a man. Therefore, the Hebrew Bible evokes the image of the stomach being moved with compassion. When we suffer with someone, we sometimes feel a pain in our gut. This is what it means to be moved by compassion. Jesus helped people because he was moved by compassion to help them, so when your gut tells you to help someone, help that person. That's walking in the steps of Jesus.

But don't wait for a feeling in your gut before you actively meet people's needs. Sometimes our feelings are fickle. They can mislead us. Sometimes genuine love means going against our feelings. It means doing what we know is right whether we feel like it or not.

When your heart goes out to someone, find a way to help that person. But be wise. Pray for insight. Figure out the best way to help.

What can we learn from Jesus' cleansing the leprosy of this man?

First, we learn that the poor are desperate for help.

In the first century, lepers were considered the walking dead. A leper was obligated to tell anyone who approached him that he was unclean. This leper was bold. His behavior was atypical of a leper. He should have kept his distance from Jesus. He should have sounded the warning, "Unclean! Unclean!" Instead, he approached Jesus, knelt before him, and made a request, "If you are willing, you can make me clean."

Why would the leper break social convention to approach Jesus in such a way? Because he was desperate. Desperation causes you to do things that aren't normal. We need to realize that we live in a world where the poor are desperate for help.

The leper's boldness demonstrates his desperation. Many of the miracle stories portray the person in need of healing as being bold: the lady with the issue of blood who reached out to touch Jesus' garment, the blind men in Jericho who would not stop crying out, "Lord, Son of David, have mercy on us." Why? Because they were desperate to get help.

Today, over 20,000 children will die due to conditions of poverty. Today, some 800 million people will go hungry. Today, around 27 million children will serve as slaves in the slave industry.

These people are desperate. We don't know their names. We may never see their faces, but they are out there.

I told the story in the introduction of visiting a Hindu temple in Calcutta, where just outside there were beggars who approached our car with hands outstretched, crying for a few rupees. These children were emaciated. You could see their ribs protruding from under their skin, which looked as thin as paper. There was a look of desperation in their eyes.

When you come face to face with the poorest of the poor, it tears your heart open. But many of us live lives that are isolated from images of the poor. We need to stay informed and understand that the world is filled with desperate people. We need to have compassionate hearts and respond to the needs of the poor and needy.

Second, we learn that Jesus responds to desperate people.

Look at Jesus' response to the leper: "Jesus was indignant. He reached out his hand and touched the man. 'I am willing,' he said. 'Be clean!' Immediately the leprosy left him and he was cleansed." I wonder if the leper felt surprised when Jesus didn't pull away from him in disgust. Surely any other rabbi would have. Any other rabbi would not have dared to touch the leper lest he become unclean. Any other rabbi would have castigated the leper for approaching him.

But Jesus was unlike any other rabbi; he did not back away—he reached out to touch him. As the hand of Jesus came closer and closer to the leper, I wonder if the leper backed away from Jesus' touch. I wonder if the leper cringed when Jesus' hand approached his skin.

Then, the touch. Jesus should have become unclean from that touch. Instead, the leper became clean.

Jesus had a different heart, a compassionate heart. He wanted to help the man. He not only healed the man's disease, but was concerned that the man reconnect with society and live a full life. So he sent him to the priest to offer a sacrifice of cleansing.

This is the heart that Jesus wants us to have. 1 Peter 2:21 states, "To this you were called, because Christ suffered for you, leaving you an example, that you should follow in his steps."

What can we do that is similar to Jesus in this situation? We can't heal the leper (or at least I can't). We can't solve all the world's problems. We can't feed every hungry person in the world today (although I am convinced that if all nations worked together to eliminate global hunger, it could be eradicated). We can't provide medicine for every sick person in the world (although I am convinced that if corporate greed turned to corporate compassion, medicine could be distributed to those who cannot afford it). It gets a bit overwhelming when you hear of all the needs that exist in the world. When I hear that over 20,000 children will die today, this overwhelms me.

So what can I do that Jesus did here? Before Jesus healed the man, he first reached out and touched him. I can give someone a warm embrace. I can give someone a touch of God's grace.

Let's get involved in making a difference in the world. Let's find a way to show compassion to people. You never know what a compassionate act might do.

ﻋﻠﻰ ﻋﻠﻰ ﻋﻠﻰ

Pay It Forward[21]

The man was elderly, unshaven, unkempt, and ragged. As he sat there, pedestrians walked by him giving him dirty looks. They clearly wanted nothing to do with him because of who he was—a dirty, homeless man.

A woman approached him. She was moved with compassion.

It was very cold that day, and the man wore a tattered coat—more like an old suit coat than a warm, winter coat—wrapped around him.

The woman stopped. She spoke. "Sir?" she asked. "Are you all right?"

The man looked up. He noticed a woman who was clearly accustomed to the finer things of life. Her coat was new. She looked like she had never missed a meal in her life. His first thought was that she wanted to make fun of him, like so many others had done before. "Leave me alone," he growled.

To his amazement, the woman continued to stand above him. She was smiling, "Are you hungry?" she asked.

"No," he answered sarcastically. "I've just come from dining with the president. Now go away."

The woman's smile became even broader. Suddenly the man felt a gentle hand under his arm. She began to lift him.

"What are you doing, lady?" the man asked angrily. "I said to leave me alone."

Just then a policeman came up. "Is there any problem, ma'am?" he asked.

"No problem here, officer," the woman answered. "I'm just trying to get this man to his feet. Will you help me?"

The officer scratched his head. "That's old Jack. He's

---

[21] I found this story at http://www.sermonillustrationlibrary.org/illustration71. I worked on it a bit. I think it illustrates how compassion moves our hearts to action. And that a good deed never goes unnoticed.

been a fixture around here for years. What do you want with him?"

"See that cafeteria over there?" the woman pointed. "I'm going to get him something to eat and get him out of the cold for a while."

"Are you crazy, lady?" the homeless man resisted. "I don't want to go in there!" Then he felt strong hands grab his other arm and lift him up.

"Let's go, Jack," said the officer.

"Let me go, officer. I didn't do anything."

"This is a good deal for you, Jack," the officer answered. "Don't blow it."

Finally, and with some difficulty, the woman and the police officer got Jack into the cafeteria. They sat him at a table in a remote corner. It was the middle of the morning, so most of the breakfast crowd had already left and the lunch bunch had not yet arrived.

The manager strode across the cafeteria and stood by the table. "What's going on here, officer?" he asked. "What is all this? Is this man in trouble?"

"This lady brought this man in here to be fed," the policeman answered.

"Not in here!" the manager replied angrily. "Having a person like that here is bad for business."

Old Jack smiled a toothless grin. "See, lady? I told you so. Now if you'll let me go. I didn't want to come here in the first place."

The woman turned to the cafeteria manager and smiled. "Sir, are you familiar with Eddy and Associates, the banking firm down the street?"

"Of course I am," the manager answered. "They hold their weekly meetings in one of my banquet rooms."

"And do you make a good amount of money providing food at these weekly meetings?"

"What business is that of yours?"

"I, sir, am Penelope Eddy, president and CEO of the

company."

"Oh."

The woman smiled again. "I thought that might make a difference." She glanced at the cop who was busy stifling a giggle. "Would you like to join us for a cup of coffee and a meal, officer?"

"No thanks, ma'am," the officer replied. "I'm on duty."

"Then, perhaps, a cup of coffee to go?"

"Yes, ma'am. That would be very nice."

The cafeteria manager turned on his heel. "I'll get your coffee for you right away, officer."

The officer watched him walk away. "You certainly put him in his place," he said.

"That was not my intent. Believe it or not, I have a reason for all this." She sat down at the table across from her amazed dinner guest. She stared at him intently. "Jack, do you remember me?"

Old Jack searched her face with his old, rheumy eyes. "I think so—I mean, you do look familiar."

"I'm older now," she said. "I've filled out since my younger days when you worked here, and I came through that very door, cold and hungry."

"Ma'am?" the officer said questioningly. "What are you saying?"

"I was just out of college," the woman began. "I had come to the city looking for a job, but I couldn't find anything. Finally I was down to my last few pennies and had been kicked out of my apartment. I walked the streets for days. It was February and I was cold and nearly starving. I saw this place and walked in on the off chance that I could get something to eat."

Jack lit up with a smile. "Now I remember," he said. "I was behind the serving counter. You came up and asked me if you could work for something to eat. I said that it was against company policy."

"I know," the woman continued. "Then you made me the biggest roast beef sandwich that I had ever seen, gave me a cup of coffee, and told me to go over to a corner table and enjoy it. I was afraid that you would get in trouble. Then, when I looked over, I saw you put money for my food in the cash register. I knew then that everything would be all right."

"So you started your own business?" Old Jack asked.

"I got a job that very afternoon. I worked my way up. Eventually I started my own business that, with the help of God, prospered." She opened her purse and pulled out a business card. "When you are finished here, I want you to pay a visit to a Mr. Lyons. He's the personnel director of my company. I'll go talk to him now, and I'm certain he'll find something for you to do around the office." She smiled. "I think he might even find the funds to give you a little advance so that you can buy some clothes and get a place to live until you get on your feet. And if you ever need anything, my door is always open for you."

There were tears in the old man's eyes. "How can I ever thank you?" he said.

"Don't thank me," the woman answered. "To God goes the glory. He led me to you."

علی علی علی

When we are compassionate to others, we demonstrate the love of Jesus who was compassionate to those in need. When we are compassionate, we become like Jesus. Why show compassion? Because Jesus did.

Think of something that you can do this week to help someone. It might be a small act of compassion. But in this small act, we become a little more like Jesus.

علی علی علی

Port-au-Prince, Haiti
GSK, 2017

I love Haiti. I LOVE Haiti.

The people are irrepressible. The disciples are beyond warm and friendly. And the mangoes! You haven't tasted a mango until you have tasted a freshly picked mango in Haiti.

Haiti is the poorest country in the Western Hemisphere. What wealth the country could have accumulated over the years was stolen by corrupt politicians.

When I travel to places like Lagos and Nairobi, the brothers say to me, "You seem to be doing okay. The heat hasn't zapped you and you are managing the crowds and traffic just fine. How is that?"

"You've never been to Haiti," I reply. "Haiti will get you ready for anything."

When my daughter Chelsea and I arrived at the home where we stayed, I saw two brothers putting together an electric fan. Later, I noticed that same fan in the bedroom that we shared. The family didn't own a fan, but they went out and bought one for us. I've found that people who don't have much are generous like that. They give you what they can't afford for themselves.

The fan worked great until the electricity went out. And the electricity went out every night. In Lagos, many people own their own generators so that when the electricity goes out, the generator kicks on. In Haiti, people can't afford generators. If they could, they couldn't afford the gas to power one.

The house where we stayed had no running water. Every couple of days a neighbor would turn on an outdoor faucet and people would stand in line to fill up buckets. They would dump this water into a larger bucket at their house. That bucket was their water supply. It provided their drinking water, water for bathing, and water for flushing toilets. Every time you needed to flush the toilet, you'd pour water into the reservoir of the toilet and you'd hope to high heaven the toilet would flush. The only time our hosts got a bit flustered with us was when we didn't flush the toilet properly. That happened more than once.

Meals were simple. Mostly vegetables. Rice and beans. Plantains. Fresh fruit. More rice. My daughter and I were vegan, so we didn't miss the meat.

It was hot and humid. But hot is okay. You adjust.

The home where we stayed was full of love. What more can you ask for than that?

Did I mention that I LOVE Haiti? It's one of my favorite places on earth. The country is poor, but its people are generous. So generous.

I am so grateful for the family that loaned us their bedroom, bought us a fan, taught us how to flush a toilet with a bucket of water, cooked us rice and beans, and fed us mangoes. You shared what you had with us. Thank you.

Chapter Eight

The Jesus Dream or the American Dream?

A rich but miserable man once visited a rabbi, seeking understanding of his life and how he might find peace. The rabbi led the man to a window and said, "What do you see?"

"I see men, women, and children," answered the rich man.

The rabbi then took the man and stood him in front of a mirror. "Now what do you see?" he asked.

"I see myself," the rich man replied.

"Yes," said the rabbi. "It is a strange thing, is it not? In the window there is a glass and in the mirror there is a glass. But the glass of the mirror is covered with a little silver, and no sooner is the silver added than you cease to see others, and see only yourself."[22]

—from *The Fast That I Choose, A Bible Study on Hunger*

علم علم علم

I must have been around twenty-two. I was working as a singles minister at Brooks Avenue Church of Christ in Raleigh, North Carolina while I pursued a master of divinity with languages degree at Southeastern Baptist Theological Seminary in Wake Forest. Another twenty-something man from the singles group at Brooks approached me and asked me for an hour of my time. Since he was in my singles group, I didn't think I could dodge him.

We met in my office.

"What would you like to talk about?" I asked.

"Close your eyes and dream with me," he said.

---

[22] *The Fast That I Choose, A Bible Study on Hunger* (Big Island, VA: Society of St. Andrew, 2009), 19.

I felt uncomfortable, but I shut my eyelids and waited for further instruction.

"What is your dream car?" he asked.

I opened my eyes.

"Close your eyes," he insisted.

I complied.

"What is your dream car?"

"I'm not really into cars," I answered. The answer was truthful. I've never been infatuated with cars. My priority in a car is that when I turn the key, it starts.

"Just dream with me," he said.

"Okay. A Grand Prix."

"Not dreamy enough," he said. "How about a Ferrari?"

"Okay."

"What color?" he asked.

"Tennessee orange."

"Not sure a Ferrari comes in that color," he said.

"It's my dream."

"Okay."

"What is your dream house?" he asked.

"I'd like a nice, comfortable four-bedroom house on an acre of land."

"Not big enough," he said. "Try again."

"I'd like a nice, comfortable six-bedroom house on two acres of land."

"Still not big enough," he said.

"Okay. I want a mansion just over the hilltop in that bright land where I'll never grow old."

"Great," he said. He didn't catch that the description of my dream house was from a Christian hymn.

"I'm not really into houses," I said.

"What are you into?" he asked.

"Books. I love books."

"Describe your dream library."

I fell into his trap. He'd found my weakness. I started spitting out a description of my dream library:

"I'd like a library that is separate from my house. I'd like my library to be built in the shape of an octagon. Four of the eight sides have large windows so light streams into the room. The floor is made of oak, lightly stained. The light of the sun bounces off the gleam of the floor and in certain spots, rainbows form.

"The ceiling is high. It's twelve feet—no, twenty feet high—no, thirty feet high. The room is the size of a gymnasium—no, a stadium. It's so big that when I turn the page of a book, the sound of the page turning echoes off the walls and then drifts into silence.

"Shelves line the walls. They are made of solid, top-grade white pine with a light tan stain. Shelves run from floor to ceiling. To reach the higher shelves there are oak ladders attached to metal runners that circle the room.

"One section of the library contains first editions of the world's great authors—all the works of Faulkner, Tolstoy, Dickens, Flaubert, Hawthorne, Dostoyevsky, Joyce and Poe; and a first printing of the Gutenberg Bible and the King James Bible of 1611.

"A special glass-encased display holds signed first editions of *The Lord of the Rings* and *The Hobbit*, plus original artwork by J. R. R. Tolkien himself. First editions of C. S. Lewis' books sit in another display.

"In a corner of the library, I'd like a massive oak table with an oak swivel chair. On the table, I'd like copies of early Greek New Testament manuscripts. I'd like p52 (the John Rylands Fragment), p46 (the Chester Beatty Papyrus), p66 (the Bodmer Papyrus), the Codex Sinaiticus, Codex Alexandrinus, Codex Vaticanus, Codex Bezae, and other early manuscripts that have yet to be catalogued.

"The room has a special thermostat that continually adjusts the climate of the space to the exact humidity, temperature, and lighting that is conducive to maintaining the longevity of museum-quality works."

"You've thought about this quite a bit," he interjected.

"And I'd like one reading chair and two reading lamps that sit precisely in the center of the octagon. I'd like the reading chair to be upholstered in plush velvet, royal blue in color. I'd like the two reading lamps to be placed on either side of the chair pointed directly at the book in my hands. I'd like the shades of the reading lamps to be made from the vellum of the Dead Sea Scrolls."

"That's it," he said. "That's a dream worth dreaming."

"Why?" I asked.

"Why what?" he retorted.

"Why are you asking me to dream about something that is unattainable?"

"That's just it," he said. "It *is* attainable."

"On a minister's salary," I quipped.

"That's why I'm here," he said. "I want to introduce you to something that is going to save America."

I listened.

"I want to give you the opportunity to be a part of a family that will help you build that library, buy that house, and drive that car. It's called the Colossal Dream Machine."[23]

I recognized the name. "CDM," I said.

"You've heard of it?" he asked.

"It's a pyramid scheme," I said. "You want me to join under you so that you'll get a percentage of everything I earn."

"No," he said. "I want to help you fulfill *your* dreams."

"No," I said. "You want me to help you fulfill *your* dreams."

"It will save America," he said.

"You've drunk the Kool-Aid," I said. "I'm not interested."

He grew agitated. "I'm offering you the chance of a lifetime."

I was calm. "For a moment there, you had me. I went down the rabbit hole with you. But when you said that your company would save America, I woke up. No one can save except Jesus."

---

[23] I changed the name of the company. As far as I know, there is no company called the Colossal Dream Machine. If you're developing a startup and have been looking for a fantastic name, look no more.

"I didn't mean it like that," he said.

I squinted my eyes and pursed my lips. "I think you did."

He rose from his chair. "Last chance."

"No thanks."

He exited my office.

I reached for my New Testament and turned to the Sermon on the Mount. I found the verse I was looking for—Matthew 6:19–21. The words were in red print:

> Do not store up for yourselves treasures on earth, where moths and vermin destroy, and where thieves break in and steal. But store up for yourselves treasures in heaven, where moths and vermin do not destroy, and where thieves do not break in and steal. For where your treasure is, there you heart will be also.

Jesus said, "For where your treasure is, there your heart will be also." This chart of American spending priorities shows us what is treasured in American culture.

America's Spending Priorities[24]

Ice cream and frozen desserts:	$23 Billion
Motion pictures:	$9.6 Billion
DVD movie rentals and purchases:	$22.4 Billion
Pet products:	$45.4 Billion
Video and computer games:	$18.8 Billion
Candy:	$23.8 Billion
Restaurants:	$566 Billion
Beer:	$91.6 Billion
Soft drinks:	$65.9 Billion

---

[24] The Fast That I Choose, 9.

Salty snack foods:	$15.9 Billion
Weight control products:	$40 Billion
Consumer electronics:	$171 Billion
Music (CDs and downloads):	$10.4 Billion
GRAND TOTAL:	**$1,103.8 Billion**

For those of us who live in suburban USA, we can easily sleepwalk through life. We have our schedules, our agendas, and we drift through life going from one appointment to the next. As the Beatles sang, "Woke up, got out of bed, dragged a comb across my head."[30] We live out one monotonous day after the next.

But God wants us to experience a full life. God wants to shake the doldrums out of our lives; he wants to sweep the cobwebs from our minds; he wants to show us what real living is all about.

When we follow Jesus, life should be an adventure. Jesus lived an adventurous life. He knew his purpose. He came to please God, to heal people, to preach the good news of God's kingdom, and to die for sin. For Jesus, every day was different. Every day was a new adventure. When we sign up to be disciples of Jesus, we sign up to live like him. This means that Jesus will alter our lives and he will alter our dreams.

Too often we buy in to the American dream. (I use the term "American dream" with the understanding that it is a global dream sought by many living outside the United States. In that sense, it is the Modern dream and encompasses the entire world.) The American dream is to better ourselves through hard work so that we can surround ourselves with material possessions. The American dream is to work hard so that we can play hard.

Very often, the American dream is a selfish dream. It comes in conflict with the Jesus dream. Which dream will we choose? To follow the dream of Jesus, it will cost us something.

In Luke 9:57–62, Jesus discusses with some prospective

---

[25] The Beatles, Lennon/McCartney, "A Day in the Life" from *Sgt. Pepper's Lonely Hearts Club Band*, EMI Studios and Regent Sound Studio, London, 1967.

followers the cost of discipleship. Three men came to Jesus seeking to follow him. He tried to talk each one of them out of it. This seems like a terrible strategy if you are trying to build a movement. People volunteer and you talk them out of volunteering. This is counterintuitive. Most recruiting centers want the prospective recruits to understand what they will receive when they sign on the dotted line. Jesus takes things in the other direction. He tells these prospective recruits, "If you are going to sign on the dotted line, this is what it will cost you."

> As they were walking along the road, a man said to him, "I will follow you wherever you go."
> Jesus replied, "Foxes have holes and birds of the air have nests, but the Son of Man has no place to lay his head."
> He said to another man, "Follow me."
> But the man replied, "Lord, first let me go and bury my father."
> Jesus said to him, "Let the dead bury their own dead, but you go and proclaim the kingdom of God."
> Still another said, "I will follow you, Lord; but first let me go back and say good-bye to my family."
> Jesus replied, "No one who puts his hand to the plow and looks back is fit for service in the kingdom of God."

Notice, the first man says, "I will follow you wherever you go." Jesus doesn't say, "Great, join in." He gives the man a warning, effectively saying, "Foxes sleep in holes, birds sleep in nests, but I have no idea where I'm sleeping tonight." That's not very encouraging. It's definitely not prosperity theology, which says that if you follow Jesus he will make your every materialistic dream come true—a nice house, a nice car, all the techno-play toys you could want. Jesus said, "I don't know where I'm spending the night, and if you follow me, you must be ready to live that kind of life."

Jesus says to another man, "Follow me." This man offers up an excuse for not following: "Lord, first let me go and bury my father." Jesus answers him, "Let the dead bury their own dead, but you go and proclaim the kingdom of God."

When someone dies, we want to be there to show our respect. When a close family member dies, we want to be there for the family. Why is Jesus so tough on this guy? Surely the mission could wait a few days or a few weeks. But Jesus says, in effect, "Let the rest of your family bury him; you go and proclaim the kingdom of God."

A third man comes to sign up for the Christian Jubilee. He says to Jesus, "I will follow you, Lord; but first let me go back and say good-bye to my family." Jesus' reply is, "No good-byes." He then says, "No one who puts his hand to the plow and looks back is fit for service in the kingdom of God."

Wow. Jesus is not making it easy on these three guys. To the first, he says, "Plan on being homeless." To the second, he says, "Let your family bury your dead father." To the third, he says, "No good-byes. Follow now or don't follow." It seems that all three didn't follow. Jesus lost three recruits that day.

We live in a culture of negotiations. We want things to be on our terms. We want everything to be a win-win. But Jesus tells these three guys, "My way or the highway." That's a counterintuitive way to start a movement.

But Jesus was being honest with these men. To follow Jesus means that we must abandon everything to follow him. When we choose to follow Jesus, we no longer pursue the American dream; we pursue the Jesus dream. To follow Jesus means that we must surrender everything to his care. To follow Jesus means that he must become everything, and we must become nothing. That is the call of discipleship. That's the nature of lordship.

Jesus is Lord, and we are his servants. Jesus is everything, and we are nothing. If we aren't ready to give up everything to follow

Jesus, then we aren't ready to be his disciples. There is simplicity in this calling. We give up everything, and we follow Jesus. We embrace a single-minded focus of seeking the kingdom first.

Look at Luke 14:25–33:

> Large crowds were traveling with Jesus, and turning to them he said: "If anyone comes to me and does not hate father and mother, wife and children, brothers and sisters—yes, even their own life—such a person cannot be my disciple. And whoever does not carry their cross and follow me cannot be my disciple.
>
> "Suppose one of you wants to build a tower. Won't you first sit down and estimate the cost to see if you have enough money to complete it? For if you lay the foundation and are not able to finish it, everyone who sees it will ridicule you, saying, 'This person began to build and wasn't able to finish.'
>
> "Or suppose a king is about to go to war against another king. Won't he first sit down and consider whether he is able with ten thousand men to oppose the one coming against him with twenty thousand? If he is not able, he will send a delegation while the other is still a long way off and will ask for terms of peace. In the same way, those of you who do not give up everything you have cannot be my disciples."

Jesus had a large crowd following him. These people were ready to enlist. Then Jesus addressed the crowd. Look at his opening line, "If anyone comes to me and does not hate his father and mother, his wife and children, his brothers and sisters—yes, even his own life—he cannot be my disciple."

Jesus let his audience know upfront what they would have to give up to be his disciples. To follow Jesus, you have to be willing to forfeit houses, material possessions, friends, and family. In case they missed how serious Jesus was, he used the word "hate." Hate father, mother, wife, children, brothers, sisters, and, yes, even your own life.

If that wasn't enough, Jesus added, "And anyone who does not carry his cross and follow me cannot be my disciple." What was the purpose of a cross? There was only one purpose for a cross in first-century Palestine—to inflict slow, torturous death on the victim.

How would we react if someone we respected as a godly, spiritual person said to us, "Sell everything you have and give it to the poor"?

These passages challenge us because they teach radical discipleship. They run counter to our culture, counter to the way we do things. Is Jesus expecting the same out of us today? Many people don't like these passages, so they try to explain them away. They say, "Jesus didn't mean the rich young man had to sell everything. He was just testing his heart." In doing this, they rewrite the text. We need to let the passage say what it is saying. Jesus was challenging the young man and us to radical discipleship in which he is Lord and in which we surrender all to him.

One writer has said that we want a Jesus created in our image. He describes this Jesus as:

> A nice, middle-class, American Jesus. A Jesus who doesn't mind materialism and who would never call us to give away everything we have. A Jesus who would not expect us to forsake our closest relationships so that he receives all our affection. A Jesus who is fine with nominal devotion that does not infringe on our comforts, because, after all, he loves us just the way we are. A Jesus who wants us to be balanced, who wants us to avoid dangerous extremes, and who, for that matter, wants us to avoid danger altogether. A Jesus who brings us comfort and prosperity as we live out our Christian spin on the American dream.[26]

[26] David Platt, *Radical: Taking Back Your Faith from the American Dream* (Portland, OR: Multnomah, 2010), 13.

But a Jesus made in our image is not the Jesus of the Bible. Jesus didn't live out the American dream. Jesus lived out the Jesus dream. Which dream are you living out in your life? Jesus calls us to abandon the American dream for his dream. He calls us to surrender our lives to him. He calls us to give up everything for him. He does this unapologetically and unabashedly. Are you willing to follow the Jesus dream?

Every day, we have a decision to make, "Are we going to pursue the American dream or the Jesus dream?" What are we going to make our priority? Jesus bids us die to self in order to follow him.

In Matthew 6:33, Jesus said, "Seek first his kingdom and his righteousness and, all these things will be given to you as well." What are the "all these things"? "All these things" include food, clothing, and housing. These are the very things that most people who are caught up in the American dream put first in their lives.

We are not to follow the American dream. Our priority must be the Jesus dream. And the Jesus dream includes compassion for those who have little or nothing.

Let me ask you a question: "What is your treasure?" Is it God's kingdom?

In Matthew 13:44, Jesus says, "The kingdom of heaven is like treasure hidden in a field. When a man found it, he hid it again, and then in his joy went and sold all he had and bought that field."

Here is the story of a man who stumbled upon a treasure while walking through a field. He looked around and made sure no one noticed his newly found treasure. He took it and hid it so that no one else would stumble upon it. Then he sold all he had and bought the field.

What did he give up to purchase the field? Everything. What did he gain by buying the field? Everything.

That's the way God works. We give up everything for God; and God gives us everything we need when we follow him. We surrender all, and we gain all.

Now read verses 45–46. Jesus said, "Again, the kingdom of heaven is like a merchant looking for fine pearls. When he found one of great value, he went away and sold everything he had and bought it."

Same story, just a different person and a different treasure, a pearl merchant who has spent all his life looking at pearls. One day he stumbled across a pearl like no other. What did he do? He sold everything he had in order to buy it. Again, he sold everything to gain everything. David Platt states:

> This brings us to the crucial question for every professing or potential follower of Jesus: What is Jesus worth to you?
>
> Do you believe he is worth abandoning everything for? Do you really believe Jesus is so good, so satisfying, and so rewarding that you will leave all you own and all you are to find your fullness in him? Do you believe him enough to obey him and to follow him wherever he leads, even when the crowds in our culture—and maybe in our churches—turn the other way?[27]

Do you believe Jesus is worth abandoning everything for? Are you willing to give up the American dream for the Jesus dream?

The treasure in the field and the pearl of great price both represent the kingdom of God. When we discover God's kingdom, we must give up everything to be part of it.

What is your treasure? Is it wrapped up in seeking the American dream? Is your dream a comfortable house, a nice car, nice schools and parks for the kids, three or four weeks of vacation per year, a Saturday morning of golf, a Saturday afternoon of football, and a juicy 401(k)?

While we pursue this dream, many around the world live in a nightmare. They live in darkness; they have no dreams—no

[27] David Platt, *The Radical Question: What Is Jesus Worth to You?* (Portland, OR: Multnomah, 2010), 50–51.

spiritual dreams and no material dreams. They live without Christ in abject poverty. Some estimate that there are over a billion people in the world who know nothing about Jesus. Imagine that—a billion people who have never heard the name of Jesus.

We must wake up and align our priorities with the priorities of Jesus.

What are we going to do different for God? What are we going to do that will make an impact for eternity? What are we going to do to help change someone else's life forever? What contribution will we give to the cause of Christ, to his eternal kingdom, to his church on earth?

مه مه مه

Beware the entanglement of wealth.

I don't know where I heard it, but I heard someone say, "The American dream might be your worst nightmare." I think that's true.

There are many warnings in the Scriptures about the deceitfulness of wealth. As you read these warnings from Scripture, you can replace "rich," "riches," "money," and "wealth" with "The American dream" or "the Modern dream."

> Don't weary yourself to be rich. In your wisdom, show restraint.
> Why do you set your eyes on that which is not? For it certainly sprouts wings like an eagle and flies in the sky.
> Proverbs 23:4–5 New English Bible

Proverbs is wisdom literature; people who follow the proverbs learn to be wise. The writer states, "Don't weary yourself to be rich" (the American dream). How many people do you know who have worked themselves to the bone, added tremendous stress to their lives, missed precious time with their families, lost opportunities to bond with their children, sacrificed their marriages, and died with money in the bank but with no spiritual legacy to pass on to others?

Chasing riches is a mirage, a trap. The writer adds, "In your wisdom, show restraint." The wise person knows that enough is enough.

Instead of wearing yourself out getting rich, pursue a spiritual legacy, which will last forever.

> Keep falsehood and lies far from me;
>> give me neither poverty nor riches,
>> but give me only my daily bread.
> Otherwise, I may have too much and disown you
>> and say, "Who is the LORD?"
> Or I may become poor and steal,
>> and so dishonor the name of my God.
>
> Proverbs 30:8–9

I love this proverb. "Give me neither poverty nor riches" (the Modern dream). Instead, help me realize when enough is enough (daily bread).

Don't allow me to be a person of extremes. It is extremely difficult to crawl out of poverty. It is just as difficult to let go of riches. Both extremes can lead to ungodly behavior. When a person is in poverty, there is the temptation to steal. When you have the Modern dream, there is the tendency to become proud, puffed up, and to act like everything you have earned is because of your own talent and ability. You lose sight of God. You devote yourself to the holy trinity of greed, "I, me, my."

Give me my daily bread. Help me to understand when enough is enough, and to be satisfied with enough. Help me to live on less than I earn so that I might have money to use for the good of others.

Allow me to honor your name by turning away from riches so that I can help others out of poverty. By doing so, I embrace the prayer, "Give me neither poverty or riches."

Whoever loves money never has enough;
> whoever loves wealth is never satisfied with their
income.
> This too is meaningless.
As goods increase,
> so do those who consume them.
And what benefit are they to the owners
> except to feast their eyes on them?
The sleep of a laborer is sweet,
> whether they eat little or much,
but as for the rich, their abundance
> permits them no sleep.

I have seen a grievous evil under the sun:
> wealth hoarded to the harm of its owners,
> or wealth lost through some misfortune,
so that when they have children
> there is nothing left for them to inherit.
Everyone comes naked from their mother's womb,
> and as everyone comes, so they depart.
They take nothing from their toil
> that they can carry in their hands.

Ecclesiastes 5:10–15

The Teacher of Ecclesiastes writes, "Whoever loves money (the American dream) never has money enough (of the American dream); whoever loves wealth (the Modern dream) is never satisfied with his income." This rings true. When our income increases, we spend more money. Before we know it, the new income isn't enough.

What if we were to decide that when we receive an increase in income, we will continue to live on the old income and use the new, surplus income to help others? What if with every increase of income our standard of living stayed the same and our benevolent contribution increased?

Imagine that at thirty you give 10% of your income to the church, but at fifty you give 25% of your income to the church and other benevolent causes. (This is called a graduated tithe. As your income increases, you give a higher percentage of your income.)

If you increase your percentage of giving as your income grows, then later in life you can build a gift-legacy through your contribution. You could start a school in a neighborhood in Haiti. You could provide clean drinking water for a village in Ethiopia. You could help fund a medical clinic in Vietnam. And you could sponsor multiple soup kitchens in your community.

If we learned to live on what we have, then the increase of our blessings could be used to help others.

The Teacher in Ecclesiastes closes with this reminder: you came into the world naked, and you'll leave naked. Whatever we earn in this world stays here, so let's use our income to do some good in our lifetime.

Jesus said, "It is easier for a camel to go through the eye of a needle than for a rich man to enter the kingdom of God" (Mark 10:25).

Have you ever seen a camel struggle to get into a gate that was built for people? It happens in the Middle East all the time. It's nearly impossible for the camel to crawl through that gate, but it doesn't keep the animal from trying. Imagine a camel trying to crawl and squeeze through your front door. It's not happening. It's comical and sad at the same time.

Yet Jesus says that it is easier for a camel to get through a small doorway than for a person who clings to the American dream to enter God's kingdom.

I don't want to stretch this analogy too far, but camels generally come with baggage. They have a hump on their backs where they store fat. If they were to get rid of fat, it wouldn't be as difficult to get through the small gate. People who pursue the American dream over the Jesus dream carry excess baggage too. I'm thinking of baggage like pride, greed, materialism, selfish ambition, idolatry, and stress. If the American dreamer were to let go of that baggage and embrace the Jesus dream, then they could enter the narrow gate to God's kingdom.

Jesus also said, "But woe to you who are rich, for you have already received your comfort" (Luke 6:24).

A woe is the equivalent of a prophetic curse. Allow me to paraphrase here, "Cursed are you who pursue the First-World dream, for you have already received your comfort." Why would a person look for comfort in the hereafter, when the here and now is so cozy and comfortable? Life in the here and now should be a bit uncomfortable because we are strangers and aliens on this earth. We sing the hymn, "This world is not my home; I'm just a-passing through." But what if this world *is* our home? What if we have all the comforts we need right here? Yes, Jesus said he came to give us life to the full (John 10:10), but does "fullness" mean luxury and riches? Fullness for Jesus included a cross, and he promises a cross for all his followers.

Let's be careful here. Wealth is deceitful. Let's make sure that when we sing, "I can't feel at home in this world anymore," that we mean it.

> But Abraham replied, "Son, remember that in your lifetime you received your good things, while Lazarus received bad things, but now he is comforted here and you are in agony."
>
> Luke 16:25

Our choices in this life have eternal consequences. In the afterlife, Abraham looked across to the rich man and said, "Remember that in your lifetime you received your good things (the Modern dream), while Lazarus received bad things." Yet in the hereafter, their roles are reversed. The rich man wakes up in agony, while poor Lazarus is comforted. Which destiny do you prefer? Your choices in your lifetime will determine your eternal destiny.

Beware the Modern dream. Beware comfort in the here and now. Choose the Jesus dream.

> But among you there must not be even a hint of sexual immorality, or of any kind of impurity, or of greed, because these are improper for God's holy people.
>
> Ephesians 5:3

Holiness is an important theme in the Bible. God is holy, and he expects his people to be holy. "Holy" can also mean "separate." God is separate from other gods. He is qualitatively different from other gods (idols). He expects his people to be separate from the nations. Jesus said to his followers, "As it is, you do not belong to the world, but I have chosen you out of the world." The call of Jesus is a call to be separate from the world, different from the world.

Paul challenges the church to be "God's holy people." How? Paul writes that in the church, "there must not be even a hint of sexual immorality, or of any kind of impurity, or of greed (the American dream)". He says, "Not … even a hint."

How much is a hint of greed? It's different for everyone. I suggest that we all need to learn the difference between "need" and "want" in our lives. Sometimes we say, "I need this or that," when in actuality, the "need" is a want. We don't "need" another pair of running shoes (I'm being vulnerable here), but we want the new Saucony Hurricanes.

Somewhere between need and want lies "a hint of greed." Define that fine line in your heart and decide not to cross it.

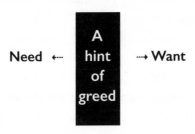

Need ⟵ **A hint of greed** ⟶ Want

> Those who want to get rich fall into temptation and a
> trap and into many foolish and harmful desires that plunge
> people into ruin and destruction. For the love of money is
> a root of all kinds of evil. Some people, eager for money,
> have wandered from the faith and pierced themselves with
> many griefs.
>
> I Timothy 6:9–10

Paul gives one of the most hard-hitting critiques of the pursuit of wealth to be found in Scripture. He begins, "Those who want to get rich fall into temptation and a trap and into many foolish and harmful desires that plunge people into ruin and destruction." Ouch. Riches are seductive. The American dream is a trap. Beware the siren call of wealth.

Then Paul warns against the love of money: "For the love of money (the First-World dream) is a root of all kinds of evil." We need money to survive in life. However, the love of money (greed, materialism) is "a root of all kinds of evil."

Paul adds a personal testimony: "Some people, eager for money (the First-World dream), have wandered from the faith and pierced themselves with many griefs." Paul doesn't mention names, but he has certain people in mind as he writes this. I sense a tone of sadness in Paul's words. These people longed for the First-World dream, but that dream turned into a nightmare. They left the faith and pierced themselves with many griefs.

Understand this—guarding your heart from the love of money is the same as protecting your life from many griefs. It's your choice.

احمد احمد احمد

Consider the words of German theologian Dietrich Bonhoeffer. Bonhoeffer lived in Germany during the time of Hitler and the rise of the Third Reich. He opposed the Third Reich and was sent to a concentration camp because of this. The day before the Allied forces liberated the camp he was in, the Nazis executed him. Bonhoeffer wrote a great book called *The Cost of Discipleship*. In this book, he states the call of Jesus as "the call to abandon the attachments of this world."[28] He writes, "When Christ calls a man, he bids him come and die."[29]

Are we willing to "come and die" in order to follow Jesus?

What do you treasure? Are you pursuing the American dream or the Jesus dream?

ﻋﻠﻰ ﻋﻠﻰ ﻋﻠﻰ

Pie in the Sky[30]
GSK

"But woe to you who are rich,
    for you have already received your comfort."
                                        —Jesus, Luke 6:24

We all want our
Pie in the sky
When we die.

But if we eat our
Pie in the sky
Before we die,
What happens to our
Pie in the sky?

If we eat our
Pie in the sky
In the here and now,

---

[28] Dietrich Bonhoeffer, *The Cost of Discipleship* (New York: Macmillan, 1966), 99.

[29] Ibid.

[30] Inspired by a poem I read once, whose author I don't recall.

What awaits us in the hereafter?

Pie here or
Pie hereafter?

Comfort here or
Comfort hereafter?

You can't have your
Pie in the sky
In the here and now and
Eat pie
In the hereafter too.

Here or hereafter?

I'll have a slice
Of lemon ice box.
To go, please.

Chapter Nine

The Sheep and the Goats

Whatsoever You Do[31]
Willard Francis Jabusch

When I was hungry, you gave me to eat.
When I was thirsty, you gave me to drink.

Whatsoever you do to the least of my brethren,
That you do unto me.
Now enter the house of my Father.

When I was homeless, you opened your doors.
When I was naked, you gave me your coat.

When I was weary, you helped me find rest.
When I was anxious, you calmed all my fears.

When I was little, you taught me to read.
When I was lonely, you gave me your love.

When in a prison, you came to my cell.
When on a sick bed, you cared for my needs.

In a strange country, you made me at home.
Seeking employment, you found me a job.

Hurt in a battle, you bound up my wounds,
Searching for kindness, you held out your hand.

---

[31] Willard Francis Jabusch, "Whatsoever You Do to the Least of My Brothers," *Catholic Book of Worship* (Ottawa, Ontario: Canadian Catholic Conference, 1972).

When I was Negro, or Chinese, or white, and
Mocked and insulted you carried my cross.

When I was aged, you bothered to smile.
When I was restless, you listened and cared.

You saw me covered with spittle and blood,
You knew my features, though grimy with sweat.

When I was laughed at, you stood by my side.
When I was happy, you shared in my joy.

ﻋﻠﻰ ﻋﻠﻰ ﻋﻠﻰ

I LOVE Matthew 25:31–46. It is one of the most grand and inspirational passages of the entire New Testament. One of my seminary professors, Dr. Richard Spencer, called it "the Mount Everest of the New Testament."[32] This passage was a foundational text for Mother Teresa, who received the Nobel Peace Prize for her ministry to the needs of the poorest of the poor in India. It has inspired many to see Jesus in the eyes of the poor and hurting.

Let's look at Matthew 25:31–46. Jesus says:

> "When the Son of Man comes in his glory, and all the angels with him, he will sit on his glorious throne. All the nations will be gathered before him, and he will separate the people one from another as a shepherd separates the sheep from the goats. He will put the sheep on his right and the goats on his left.
>
> "Then the King will say to those on his right, 'Come, you who are blessed by my Father; take your inheritance, the kingdom prepared for you since the creation of the world. For I was hungry and you gave me something to eat, I was thirsty and you gave me something to drink, I was a

---

[32] Taken from notes in Dr. Richard Spencer's New Testament Survey class at Southeastern Baptist Theological Seminary in 1983.

stranger and you invited me in, I needed clothes and you clothed me, I was sick and you looked after me, I was in prison and you came to visit me.'

"Then the righteous will answer him, 'Lord, when did we see you hungry and feed you, or thirsty and give you something to drink? When did we see you a stranger and invite you in, or needing clothes and clothe you? When did we see you sick or in prison and go to visit you?'

"The King will reply, 'Truly I tell you, whatever you did for one of the least of these brothers and sisters of mine, you did for me.'

"Then he will say to those on his left, 'Depart from me, you who are cursed, into the eternal fire prepared for the devil and his angels. For I was hungry and you gave me nothing to eat, I was thirsty and you gave me nothing to drink, I was a stranger and you did not invite me in, I needed clothes and you did not clothe me, I was sick and in prison and you did not look after me.'

"They also will answer, 'Lord, when did we see you hungry or thirsty or a stranger or needing clothes or sick or in prison, and did not help you?'

"He will reply, 'Truly I tell you, whatever you did not do for one of the least of these, you did not do for me.'

"Then they will go away to eternal punishment, but the righteous to eternal life."

In verse 31, Jesus states, "When the Son of Man comes in his glory ..." "Son of Man" was Jesus' favorite title to use of himself. It displayed his humanity. It is understood in some Old Testament passages as just another word for man. Ezekiel used it to show the ordinary nature of the prophet as a man, but also the greatness of his call and service. Jesus loved to find ways to connect with people. Thus, he often used the title—Son of Man.

The word "throne" is used in Semitic literature to symbolize authority and power. The provocative claim of Jesus here is that he will sit alone upon the throne of glory and judge the world. This concept is without parallel in biblical literature, and it demonstrates the high Christology of Matthew. Matthew demonstrates that Jesus is King. At the end of time, Jesus will sit on his throne as the King, and he will judge the world.

In verse 32, "all the nations" can also be translated "all Gentiles." The term refers to all humanity. "Gathering together" and "separating" are terms used in shepherding. The shepherd here is the keeper of a mixed herd of sheep and goats. Concerning their separation, New Testament theologian Joachim Jeremias writes, "The sheep and the goats would feed together during the day, but the shepherd would separate them at night because goats are more susceptible to cold and have to be kept warmer than sheep, which like fresh air at night."[33] Thus, shepherds would separate the sheep from the goats every night.

The sheep represent the saved because of their helplessness and absolute dependence upon the shepherd. The right side is a place of honor in Jewish literature; therefore, the sheep are placed on the right.

In verses 34–36, the king offers the inheritance of a kingdom prepared from the foundations of the world to those who minister to the needy as if they were serving Jesus. To "inherit" is to enter into the possession and enjoyment of something.

اَلَـ, اَلَـ, اَلَـ

Jesus gives a list of acts of charity in verses 35–36. He states, "For I was hungry and you gave me food, I was thirsty and you gave me drink, I was a stranger and you welcomed me, I was sick and you cared for me, I was in prison and you visited me."

The acts of charity in this list are based upon Jewish acts of charity, but the list neglects two acts which were looked upon

---

[33] Joachim Jeremias, *"poikilos, polupoikilos"* in *Theological Dictionary of New Testament,* vol. VI, edited by Gehard Kittel and Gerhard Friedrick, translated by Geoffrey W. Bromiley (Grand Rapids: Wm. B. Eerdmans, 1968), 493.

highly by the rabbis: to lament for the dead and to bury the dead. This suggests that Jesus is more concerned for the living than the dead. The rabbis did not include visiting prisoners in their lists, and Jesus' inclusion of it is probably foreshadowing Christian persecution and imprisonment.

Those who performed the acts of love for the poor were surprised that they had ministered to Jesus. This is the "gotcha" point in the story.

The King declares, "I tell you the truth, when you did it to one of the least of these brothers of mine, you did it to me."

The hardhearted servants demand to know, "When? When did we not serve you?" They ask, "Lord, when did we see you hungry or thirsty or a stranger or naked or sick or in prison, and did not care for you?"

He repeats himself, "I tell you truthfully, when you did not do it for one of the least of these, you did not do it for me."

When we serve the poor, we serve Jesus. When we turn away from meeting the needs of the poor, we turn away from Jesus.

That's the "gotcha" point of the story. Did it "getcha"?

It gets me every time I read it.

ﻋﻠﻲ ﻋﻠﻲ ﻋﻠﻲ

[Warning: I get a tiny bit technical here. So if you wish, you can skip to the next section.]

The key issue for some in the passage is found in verses 40 and 45. In verse 40, the Son of Man says, "When you did it to one of the least of these brothers of mine, you did it to me." In verse 45, the Son of Man declares, "I tell you truthfully, when you did not do it for one of the least of these, you did not do it for me." When we compare these two verses, it raises several questions. Who did Jesus refer to as "these brothers of mine" in verse 40? Who are "the least" in verse 45? Why did Jesus say not say "my brothers" in verse 45? Why did he only say "the least"?

Let's tackle the first question: to whom did Jesus refer in verse

40 as "these brothers of mine"? There are three popular answers to this question.

First, "my brothers" refers to anyone in the covenant community of Israel. This was the typical manner in which a Jewish reader would have understood the term. And, since the gospel was written for Jewish readers, it would make since to read "my brothers" as referring to Jews.

Second, another view identifies "the least of these" as Jesus' disciples. Jesus speaks of disciples as brothers in Matthew 12:48–50 and 28:10. In Matthew 10:40–42, Jesus sends out his disciples to preach, and mentions that whoever receives them in turn receives him. Also, in Matthew 24 and 25, Jesus is speaking to his disciples when he delivers his teaching on judgment and the end of time.

Therefore, Jesus uses "my brothers" to refer to disciples. His followers will be judged based on how they respond to the needs of other brothers and sisters within the community of Jesus. Craig L. Blomberg, in his amazing book, *Neither Poverty nor Riches,* advocates this position. He writes:

> Today, however, the prevailing interpretation is that Jesus is teaching about the need to help the dispossessed whether or not they are Christian. ... This is obviously an important biblical theme, but is far less likely to be the focus of this particular passage, given the consistent meaning of the terms and the larger context of parables focusing on the disciples (24:43–25:46).[34]

A third option attempts to look at the full theology of Matthew. It considers the context of Matthew's gospel as a whole. In Matthew 5:43–48 the command is given by Jesus to love one's enemies. This runs counter to the type of localized, segregated, and distinctive love which is expressed when one equates "my

---

[34] Craig L. Blomberg *Neither Poverty nor Riches: A Biblical Theology of Possessions.* (Downers Grove, IL: InterVarsity, 1999).

brothers" with disciples.

Which of these last two positions is more tenable? It's difficult to say. When we consider the whole of Matthew's theology, he is careful not to demonstrate love and righteousness with a bias. It seems the third position is preferable.

Let's attempt to answer the last two questions. Why did Jesus not say "my brothers" in verse 45? Why did he only say "the least"? There are two positions here.

First, since Jesus already said "my brothers" in verse 40, so he did not need to repeat that phrase in verse 45; it was implied. This is a sound position.

Second, Jesus did not repeat "my brothers" because he wanted to emphasize that a righteous person responds to the needs of anyone who is hungry, naked, or sick. Thus, "the least" can be those outside the covenant community of Israel. Paul S. Minias comments:

> Jesus' parable does not measure "leastness" in terms of economic destitution alone, but includes social dereliction as well. There are sick people; in the Bible sickness connotes sin and contagion. There are naked people; in the Bible nakedness connoted powerlessness and disgrace. More important still, the parable mentions strangers and convicts. These least are folk who are overlooked or ostracized, who possess no significance, prestige, or power.[35]

Minias and others believe that Jesus did not repeat "my brothers" because he wanted to emphasize that the righteous respond to anyone and everyone in need, whether that person is in the covenant community or not.

Which position is correct? Again, it's difficult to say. If you understand "my brothers" to mean anyone in need, then the question of who are "the least" is moot. However, if you understand

---

[35] Paul S. Minias, "The Coming of the Son of Man," *Theology Today IX* (October 1952); 490.

"my brothers" to mean disciples of Jesus, then the answer to who are "the least" makes a difference in how the passage is understood. Honestly, in my mind, it seems that "my brothers" would be implied in verse 45.

However, I vacillate on my understanding of this passage. There are days when I believe the correct view is to understand "my brothers" as referring to fellow disciples (primarily because of the context of Matthew 24 and 25). Other days, I believe "the least" refers to anyone who is in need, regardless of their religious, ethnic, or social background, primarily because of the wider context of Matthew's gospel, but also because Jesus ministered to Jews, Gentiles, and Samaritans.

಩಩಩

Whichever position is taken, we must understand that this is not Jesus' only teaching on this topic. This passage must be compared with other passages, like the Parable of the Good Samaritan and the teaching of Jesus on loving our enemies. In addition, there is the example of Jesus himself. He helped people outside of the covenant community of Israel—his compassion was not limited to Israel. Thus, by example, Jesus demonstrates that we are to meet the needs of anyone who is hurting.

I just spent much ink and paper discussing who Jesus is speaking of when he says "my brothers" or "the least," when in actuality his emphasis is on who *did* and *did not* help others who were hungry, thirsty, a stranger, sick, or in prison. Jesus wants us to *help others*. Helping others doesn't come from talk—it comes from action! Jesus expects his people to be people of *action*.

When we face Jesus in judgment, he will not separate the sheep from the goats based upon their interpretation of "my brothers" and "the least." Jesus will look at the sheep and say, "For I was hungry and you gave me food, I was thirsty and you gave me drink, I was a stranger and you welcomed me, I was sick and you cared for me, I was in prison and you visited me." He will say, "You

DID something for the hungry, the thirsty, the stranger, the sick, and those in prison." That's the real difference between the sheep and the goats: it's ACTION. The sheep DID; the goats DID NOT.

Conclusion

This judgment scene gives the disciples of Jesus a revelation as to what God means for his people to be. If a person strives for righteousness, then he must pay strict attention to the lesson taught in this passage. William Barclay writes, "The lesson is this—that God will judge us in accordance with our reaction to human needs."[36]

Our concept of a relationship with God can get warped when it is based on traditional standards of what it means to be a Christian. We can forget the example of Jesus and his definition of righteousness. New Testament professor Malcolm Tolbert comments:

> Sometimes we equate faithfulness to Jesus with attendance on religious services and giving money to support the institution. We honor Jesus who never said anything at all about building buildings by erecting larger and more magnificent structures. If we do take his words seriously, we shall surely testify to it by a shift of our emphasis from statistics and buildings to people in their need. The Lord is not going to ask, "How many buildings did you build?" According to the passage, he is going to ask: "How many hungry people did you feed? How many sick people did you visit?"[37]

Jesus' words should help us focus our gaze on the helpless, poor, and suffering.

Whenever we find it difficult to get out of ourselves and meet the needs of others, Jesus' words should come ringing into our

---

[36] William Barclay, *New Testament Words* (London: SCM, 1964), 36–37.

[37] Malcolm O. Tolbert, *Good News from Matthew* (Nashville: Broadman, 1975), 213.

ears. Dr. Martin Luther King, Jr. wrote:

> When we, through compassionless detachment and arrogant individualism fail to respond to the needs of the underprivileged, the Master says, "Inasmuch as ye have done it not to one of the least of these my brethren, ye have done it not unto me."[38]

As Mother Teresa states, we search and find the eyes of Jesus in every poor and helpless person.

Even though we look for the poor and rejected person, the true Christians are not searching to gain credit for themselves. Christian service is uncalculating. We should be able to ask, "Lord, when did we see you in need?" Human suffering should awaken our compassion to the point of service, but our motives should be to minister and help without any ulterior motive. Our response to the needy must be instinctive within our own Christian character for it to be pleasing to God.

ﻋﻠﻴﻪ ﻋﻠﻴﻪ ﻋﻠﻴﻪ

On Finding God[39]
Toyohiko Kagawa

> God dwells among the lowliest of men. He sits on the dust heap among the prison convicts. With the juvenile delinquents. He stands at the door, begging bread. He throngs with the beggars at the place of alms. He is among the sick. He stands in line with the unemployed in front of the free employment bureaus.
>
> Therefore, let him who would meet God visit the prison cell before going to the temple. Before he goes to

---

[38] Martin Luther King, *Strength to Love* (Glasgow: William Collins, Sons, 1964), 19.

[39] Toyohiko Kagawa, *Meditations,* translated by Jiro Takenaka (New York: Harper and Brothers, 1950), 213.

church, let him visit the hospital. Before he reads his Bible, let him help the beggar standing at his door.

If he visits the prison after going to the temple, does he not by so much delay his meeting with God? If he goes first to the church then to the hospital, does he not by so doing postpone beholding God? If he fails to help the beggar at his door and indulges himself in Bible reading, there is a danger that God, who lives among men, will go elsewhere. In truth, he who forgets the unemployed forgets God.

Eyes
GSK

Someone looks and sees the tears of loneliness
 As they trickle down from the corners of
 Bright blue eyes.

Another gazes and sees the cold, blank,
 Disease-ridden stare of death in
 Dark brown eyes.

Still another looks and wipes crusted
 Sleep from brilliant, newborn,
 Hazel eyes.

And someone stares into dimly lit,
 Uncontrolled and functionless,
 Almost colorless eyes.

Look closer into these eyes.
 Someone looks back.

And they call him Jesus.

Chapter Ten

Simplicity

Keep falsehood and lies far from me;
> give me neither poverty nor riches,
> but give me only my daily bread.
Otherwise, I may have too much and disown you
> and say, "Who is the LORD?"
Or I may become poor and steal,
> and so dishonor the name of my God.

Proverbs 30:8–9

If you look carefully you will see that there is one thing and only one thing that causes unhappiness. The name of that thing is Attachment. What is an attachment? An emotional state of clinging caused by the belief that without some particular thing or some person you cannot be happy.

—Anthony de Mello

Simplicity is freedom. Duplicity is bondage. Simplicity brings joy and balance. Duplicity brings anxiety and fear.[40]

—Richard Foster

If anyone ever lived a simple life, it was Jesus of Nazareth. His life makes Henry David Thoreau look like a hedonist. Yes, Jesus came eating and drinking, but he also did not have a home to live in or a bed to sleep in. He depended on the generosity of others while he focused on meeting the needs of people around him. His life was a simple life.

---

[40] Richard Foster, *Celebration of Discipline* (San Francisco: HarperCollins, 1988), 79.

Simplicity or frugality is the spiritual discipline where a person makes a conscious decision to trim back and get rid of excesses. When we simplify our lives, we cut out the clutter, the static, and the duplicity of life. Simplicity is about our lifestyles, but more importantly, it is about heart and attitude. We need to ask ourselves, "What do I really value in life?" and also, "What do I treasure?"

Jesus and Simplicity

In Matthew 6:19–21, Jesus states:

> Do not store up for yourselves treasures on earth, where moth and rust destroy, and where thieves break in and steal. But store up for yourselves treasures in heaven, where moth and rust do not destroy, and where thieves do not break in and steal. For where your treasure is, there your heart will be also.

In spite of this warning from Jesus, much of our lives are consumed by storing up treasures on earth. Ultimately, all these treasures are going to be expended. They won't last. But right now they sure look shiny, new, fresh, and valuable.

Where our treasures are, that's where we place our focus. I had a friend once who started investing in the stock market. He would study the market every day to see if he needed to buy or sell stock. His investments consumed him. I'd go over to his house, and he'd have the stock reports going across his television. His moods were governed by how his investments were doing. His treasure became his focus. Or perhaps, what he focused on became his treasure.

This can happen to any of us. What we invest in, we value. It takes our focus. So here's my question: Why don't we invest in the kingdom and let the kingdom be our focus?

Jesus makes it clear that where our treasure is, our heart will be there also. So where we find our treasure, we will find our heart.

Or, where our heart is, we will find our treasure. They go hand in glove.

What is your passion? What do you dream about? Where does most of your time and energy go? If you asked your closest friends what makes you really happy, what would they say? If you asked your acquaintances at school or work, what would they say? It is difficult for us to think about the hereafter and very easy for us to think of the here and now that we have in our faces all day long: "Buy this! See this! Read this! Wear this!" Focusing on the here and now steals our focus away from the hereafter.

Jesus shows us the temporal nature of treasures on earth by pointing out that moth and rust consume them and thieves break in and steal them. During Jesus' day, elaborate clothing was often used as currency, but moths easily destroyed this treasure. Precious metal was also used as currency, but rust tarnished this metal, causing it to lose its value. Houses were made of mud brick, and thieves broke through these mud brick walls and stole valuable possessions.

In our day, earthly treasures are just as temporary. Styles change overnight. We hide our money in bank safes and watch inflation eat away at it. The stock market is terribly fickle. The only really secure place to store our treasure is in heaven. In heaven nothing can get at our treasure—not moth, rust, thieves, inflation, stock market scams, or even the taxman.

Jesus is not against having a savings account or saving for your child's college education. He is not against planning for the future with a retirement fund. He warns not to store up treasure "for yourselves," implying storing selfishly. He also warns against storing up for self and leaving God out of the picture. The disciple gives first to God and uses what is left in a wise way.

In the Parable of Bigger Barns, Jesus tells the story of a man who stores up his treasure on earth. He emphasizes the futility of such a quest.

Today we might call this man a hoarder. He couldn't let go of things, so he built bigger barns. Perhaps you've heard of Homer and Langley Collyer. They lived together on the Upper West Side of Manhattan. They were famous hoarders, so famous that E. L. Doctorow wrote a book based on them entitled *Homer & Langley.* On March 21, 1947, the police went to the Collyers' house because of an anonymous phone call reporting a dead body in the house. Sure enough, after crawling through junk and debris, a policeman found the body of Homer Collyer. But where was Langley? The authorities removed over 130 tons of junk from the home. After two weeks of removing junk from the house, the police found Langley Collyer's body about ten feet from where they had found Homer's body. Langley's body was partly decomposed and eaten by rats. It was determined that he was crawling to bring food to his brother when stacks of newspaper and other debris fell on him and pinned him to the floor. He laid on that spot and starved to death. Homer and Langley couldn't build bigger barns, so they stacked stuff on top of other stuff until the stuff snuffed out their lives.

After the 130 tons of junk was removed from the house of Homer and Langley, the salvageable items were sold. Their sale only brought in $2,000. There was the body of a Model T Ford, fourteen pianos, and two organs. After the house was cleared of the junk, it was deemed a fire hazard and destroyed.

That's an extreme story, but it echoes the sentiment of the Parable of Bigger Barns. It is possible to get buried beneath our stuff. We need to look at how we view material possessions.

Preceding the parable, a man asks Jesus to settle a dispute between him and his brother concerning an inheritance. It is quite common for family members to fight over inheritances. Just within these last couple of weeks I heard of three cases where this happened. I've heard it said, "Whenever there is an inheritance, ninety-nine percent of the people become wolves." Greed gets the better of us, and we forget that we are family.

Jesus was asked to settle the dispute because he was a rabbi. The man addressed him as "Teacher." It was common in the first century for a rabbi to step in and settle this type of issue. But Jesus wasn't that kind of rabbi. He wasn't just going to step in and decide who should get what. He was going to speak to the heart of the matter. That's what Jesus does—he speaks to the heart. At the heart of the issue sat the old sin that dogs so many people: greed.

Greed, simply put, is the desire to have more. Enough doesn't satisfy. Greed wants more, more, more.

That is the context of this parable that Jesus told to illustrate the insidious nature of greed. Before he launched into the story, he said, "Watch out! Be on your guard against all kinds of greed; a man's life does not consist in the abundance of his possessions."

After the parable, Jesus taught directly concerning greed and hoarding possessions, some of the same lessons he taught in the Sermon on the Mount in Matthew 6. Jesus said, "Life is more than food, and the body more than clothes." He added, "Do not set your heart on what you will eat or drink; do not worry about it." He closed the discussion with a very direct command:

> "Sell your possessions and give to the poor. Provide purses for yourselves that will not wear out, a treasure in heaven that will not be exhausted, where no thief comes near and no moth destroys. For where your treasure is, there your heart will be also."
>
> Luke 12:33–34

The context is clear: Jesus warned his followers about the sin of greed. Possessions in themselves are not wrong; but when we become greedy for possessions, we sin.

In Matthew 19:16–30 is the story of the Rich Young Ruler. The story reads:

> Just then a man came up to Jesus and asked, "Teacher, what good thing must I do to get eternal life?"
>
> "Why do you ask me about what is good?" Jesus

replied. "There is only One who is good. If you want to enter life, keep the commandments."

"Which ones?" he inquired.

Jesus replied, "'You shall not murder, you shall not commit adultery, you shall not steal, you shall not give false testimony, honor your father and mother,' and 'love your neighbor as yourself.'"

"All these I have kept," the young man said. "What do I still lack?"

Jesus answered, "If you want to be perfect, go, sell your possessions and give to the poor, and you will have treasure in heaven. Then come, follow me."

When the young man heard this, he went away sad, because he had great wealth.

Then Jesus said to his disciples, "Truly I tell you, it is hard for someone who is rich to enter the kingdom of heaven. Again I tell you, it is easier for a camel to go through the eye of a needle than for someone who is rich to enter the kingdom of God."

When the disciples heard this, they were greatly astonished and asked, "Who then can be saved?"

Jesus looked at them and said, "With man this is impossible, but with God all things are possible."

Peter answered him, "We have left everything to follow you! What then will there be for us?"

Jesus said to them, "Truly I tell you, at the renewal of all things, when the Son of Man sits on his glorious throne, you who have followed me will also sit on twelve thrones, judging the twelve tribes of Israel. And everyone who has left houses or brothers or sisters or father or mother or wife or children or fields for my sake will receive a hundred times as much and will inherit eternal life. But many who are first will be last, and many who are last will be first."

The story of the Rich Young Ruler is found in all three gospels. The Synoptics describe him as a rich man. Luke calls him a ruler, and Matthew mentions that he is young. Thus the designation, the Rich Young Ruler.

In Mark 10, the young man approached Jesus and said, "Good teacher." In Matthew, he said, "Teacher, what good thing must I do?" Jesus responded in Mark by saying, "Why do you call me good?" and in Matthew by saying, "Why do you ask me about what is good?"

The natural way to harmonize the two accounts is to picture the rich man asking the question with the adjective "good" in both sections. For example, "Good teacher, what good thing must I do to inherit eternal life?" Jesus would have responded to both questions, "Why do you call me good, and why do you ask me what is good? Don't you know that God alone is good?"

The man came to Jesus wanting to know what to do to inherit eternal life. He had kept the commandments, so he must have been looking for something beyond the commandments that would guarantee his salvation. Jesus let him know that he was thinking incorrectly. The only "good" thing you could do to inherit eternal life was to know the "good" Father who gives eternal life. The young man was looking for a legalistic approach to God. Jesus told the man that salvation is a matter of relationship, not works.

Since Jesus is God, why does he not accept the designation of "good" as applied to him by the rich young ruler? Jesus deflected the glory that the man wanted to give him and gave it to God the Father. This was the nature of Jesus; he lived to glorify the Father. He could have accepted the designation "good," but he glorified God the Father with the title.

The fact that we have a relationship with the good Father means we must keep his commandments. When the young man asked, "What must I do," Jesus responded by listing the sixth, seventh, eighth, ninth, and fifth commandments and adding "love your neighbor as yourself."

The young man was quick to check these off his legalistic works list. "I've done all of these since I was a boy," he responded.

Jesus went straight to the man's heart. He said, "If you want to be perfect ..." "Perfect" means complete. If you want to have a complete relationship with God, then you must do this.

What is keeping you from being close to God? What is hindering your relationship with the Father? For the rich young ruler, Jesus puts his finger on the heart of the issue and says, "Go, sell your possessions and give to the poor."

The rich young ruler was unwilling to check this item off his legalistic checklist because it was the real issue that was keeping him from having a great relationship with God. D.A. Carson writes:

> He was willing to discipline himself to observe all the outward stipulations and even perform supererogatory works; but because of his wealth, he had a divided heart. His money was competing with God; and what Jesus everywhere demands as a condition for eternal life is absolute, radical discipleship. This entails the surrender of self.[41]

Riches were on the throne of his life, and since riches were sitting on the throne, God could not be on the throne. The man loved riches more than God.

In his teachings, Jesus issued more than a few warnings against greed, the abundance of possessions, wealth, riches, and selfishness. Note the following scriptures:

> Then he said to them, "Watch out! Be on your guard against all kinds of greed; a man's life does not consist in the abundance of his possessions."
>
> Luke 12:15

---

[41] D.A. Carson, *The Expositor's Bible Commentary with the New International Version* (Grand Rapids, MI: Zondervan, 1995), 424.

Then Jesus said to his disciples: "Therefore I tell you, do not worry about your life, what you will eat; or about your body, what you will wear. For life is more than food, and the body more than clothes. Consider the ravens: They do not sow or reap, they have no storeroom or barn; yet God feeds them. And how much more valuable you are than birds! Who of you by worrying can add a single hour to your life? Since you cannot do this very little thing, why do you worry about the rest?

"Consider how the wild flowers grow. They do not labor or spin. Yet I tell you, not even Solomon in all his splendor was dressed like one of these. If that is how God clothes the grass of the field, which is here today, and tomorrow is thrown into the fire, how much more will he clothe you—you of little faith! And do not set your heart on what you will eat or drink; do not worry about it. For the pagan world runs after all such things, and your Father knows that you need them. But seek his kingdom, and these things will be given to you as well.

"Do not be afraid, little flock, for your Father has been pleased to give you the kingdom. Sell your possessions and give to the poor. Provide purses for yourselves that will not wear out, a treasure in heaven that will never fail, where no thief comes near and no moth destroys. For where your treasure is, there your heart will be also."

Luke 12:22–34

"No servant can serve two masters. Either he will hate the one and love the other, or he will be devoted to the one and despise the other. You cannot serve both God and Money."

The Pharisees, who loved money, heard all this and were sneering at Jesus. He said to them, "You are the ones who justify yourselves in the eyes of others, but God knows your hearts. What people value highly is detestable in God's sight."

Luke 16:13–15

When you consider all these verses together, it's a sweeping condemnation of the first-world materialistic mindset.

What is the antidote for materialism? Simplicity.

Developing a Perspective on Material Possessions

We can own things, but we have to make certain things don't own us. There is nothing wrong with having possessions. They can be used to serve God. There is nothing wrong with money, but we need to guard against the love of money.

Paul wrote two letters to his young apprentice Timothy. In the first one, he gave instructions concerning the rich in the church, so the early church had members who were wealthy. Paul did not instruct Timothy to command these wealthy members to give up their fortunes and become poor. Paul said, "Command those who are rich to be generous." Wealth and possessions can be used in a positive way to help other people and advance God's cause.

Possessions are neutral. Scratch that. ~~Possessions are neutral.~~

Possessions that are held onto loosely and used for the benefit of others are a blessing. Possessions that are accumulated for selfish reasons are a curse. If your wealth doesn't extend beyond the personal use of your possessions, that is extremely dangerous. When possessions are used to benefit others, the person who uses their possessions in this way is considered benevolent. Belongings can also be hoarded and selfishly accumulated. The person who clings to them this way is considered greedy. What is the difference here? It's not the possessions; it's the heart.

We must guard our hearts against the love of owning things.

Beware and be aware of advertising. The point of most advertising is to get you to desire some "thing" to the point that you feel you have to have it. More than likely you don't need the item, but the objective is to make you feel that life would be incomplete without it. Richard Foster writes, "The mass media have convinced us that to be out of step with fashion is to be out of step with reality. It is time we awaken to the fact that conformity to a sick society is to be sick."[42] Amen.

I'm writing about simplifying our lives, not in order to de-clutter but so that we can help other people. If we are clearing our closets of old clothes only to restock with new clothes, what are we doing? I've heard people say, "Every time I buy something new I get rid of something old." That saves on space, but it's not the discipline of simplicity. Perhaps we should think of not buying anything new for ourselves so that we can buy something new for someone who doesn't have anything new. The call of Jesus is not the call to declutter. It's a call to live a radical life that is concerned with meeting the needs of others.

What Is Simplicity?

Simplicity is learning to live on less so we can have more—not more things, but a more abundant life in Christ. Simplicity is learning to live on less so that others can have a little something. How can we simplify our lives?

- Ask: Are there things in my life that complicate it but don't add enjoyment to life? Are there things that cause me anxiety and worry? If so, get rid of these things.

- Perhaps there are certain possessions you do enjoy but can't afford. Get rid of these things too.

- Ask: Do I buy items on impulse or on a whim? Resist this urge. If it isn't a need, don't spend the money on it. Ask yourself, will I still need this in a month, in a year? Is what you are about to purchase a want or a need?

- Learn to determine the difference between want and need.

- Learn to give stuff away. But don't do this only to clear

---

[42] Foster, *Celebration of Discipline*, 81.

space around the house or apartment. Give from your surplus to people who have little to nothing.

- Give back to the community. Get involved in volunteering. When we help people who are less fortunate than we are, it enables us to see our materialism and greed.

- Educate yourself to the plight of poverty. Learn about the lives of the poor. Whenever I return to the US after staying a week or two in a third-world country, I always feel disgusted with all the stuff I have in my life. Unfortunately, that feeling soon wears off. I have to keep scriptures on greed and materialism in front of me. Which leads me to another bullet point:

- Memorize scriptures on greed and materialism.

Too often, we measure our happiness in terms of things. What car do we drive? What clothes do we wear? What house do we live in? What education do we have?

Do we realize that the more stuff we accumulate, the more time, care, and maintenance we must put into that stuff? When we accumulate, the stuff begins to take over our lives. Over time, our lives become stuffed with stuff. Perhaps it is time to go the other direction, to de-accumulate. Perhaps it is time to de-stuff our lives.

The discipline of simplicity teaches us that joy does not come from an abundance of things. True satisfaction comes from knowing Jesus as Lord. To gain everything in Jesus, we must give up everything for him.

Simplify life.

Be generous.

Give to meet the needs of others.

Discover the freedom of simplicity.

Richard Foster's Ten Controlling Principles for the Outward Expression of Simplicity[43]

First, buy things for their usefulness rather than their status.

Second, reject anything that is producing an addiction in you.

Third, develop a habit of giving away things. ... De-accumulate.

Fourth, refuse to be propagandized by the custodians of modern gadgetry.

Fifth, learn to enjoy things without owning them.

Sixth, develop a deeper appreciation for the creation.

Seventh, look with healthy skepticism at all "buy now, pay later" schemes.

Eighth, obey Jesus' instructions about plain, honest, speech.

Ninth, reject anything that breeds the oppression of others.

Tenth, shun anything that distracts you from seeking first the kingdom of God.

'Tis the Gift to Be Simple[44]
Old Shaker hymn

'Tis the gift to be simple,
'Tis the gift to be free,
'Tis the gift to come down where you ought to be.
And when we find ourselves in the place just right,
'Twill be in the valley of love and delight.

When true simplicity is gained,
To bow and to bend we shan't be ashamed.
To turn, turn will be our delight
'Till by turning, turning we come 'round right.

---

[43] Richard J. Foster, *Celebration of Discipline* (San Francisco: HarperCollins, 1988), 90–95.
[44] In the public domain.

ة، ة، ة،

Prayer

Dear Father,

When I look around at my life, I see so much stuff. My life is filled with clutter. I pray that I will learn the joy and freedom of simplicity. Help me to de-accumulate. Help me to declutter my life. Give me a heart that is drawn to you and not to things. Help me to see that the American dream can become the American nightmare. Don't allow me to be possessed by possessions. Instead, may my heart be consumed by love for you and you alone.

In Him,

Amen

ة، ة، ة،

Three Wishes[45]
by GSK

Sometimes my family takes a vacation at Long Beach Island on the Jersey Shore.

I don't like beaches in the summer. They are hot, sandy, and filled with partially naked bodies. However, I don't mind beaches in winter. They are cold, still sandy, and if a body is on the beach, it's clothed.

I was walking along the Jersey Shore in late February when I tripped over a bottle. I'd seen this type of bottle before in pictures. Not photographs, but drawings and paintings in various books. It was a genie's bottle.

What do you do when you find a genie's bottle? You rub it. So I did.

Poof. Out popped a genie.

"You have three wishes," the genie said.

---

[45] Inspired by "The October Tale," a story by Neil Gaiman in *A Calendar of Tales*, http://www.acalendaroftales.com/.

"No proper introduction?" I asked, offering my hand for a shake.

"I was reading Harry Potter when you summoned me, and I'd like to get back to the story. You have three wishes, and you can't wish for a thousand more wishes. It doesn't work that way. Only three."

"But I always thought that if I were given three wishes, my first wish would be for a thousand more wishes and my second wish would be for a wish meter to keep up with my wishes."

"I get that a lot. It doesn't work that way."

"Can I gift my wishes to other people?" I asked.

"Are you serious?"

"Yes."

"I've been around since Salah al-Din ibn Ayyub, and no one has ever asked me if they could give away their wishes."

"Who?"

"Perhaps you know him as Saladin?"

"Doesn't ring a bell."

"Defeated the Crusaders at the battle of the Horns of Hattin on July 4, 1187."

"Still no bell," I paused. "Wow. You *are* old."

"Yes. And you have three wishes."

"Can they be gifted?"

His face grew agitated. "I must check the manual."

Poof. The genie was gone.

I took a seat on the sand and looked out at the calming waves. "Three wishes," I said out loud. No one heard me. I was alone on the beach.

Poof. The genie appeared.

"I checked the manual. Your wishes can be gifted. But I don't recommend it. I recommend that you use your wishes to secure your future. Property is a nice investment. You can't go wrong with gold. Children? Do you have children? Perhaps you'd like to use a wish on your children?"

"I do have children," I said. "But I want them to earn what they get in life. And I have enough stuff in my life. No need for property or gold."

"You have enough," the genie said. "No one has ever said that to me. Usually people can't wait to wish for more things, more possessions, more stuff."

"And that's your trap," I said.

"What?" The genie feigned being hurt.

"I know who Salah al-Din ibn Ayyub was, and I've been to the Horns of Hattin in Galilee. I also know that genies, or jinn, are notoriously evil and love to entrap witless humans with their three wishes. It's how you get your kicks. However, I was happily surprised that you were reading Harry Potter."

"Truth be known," the genie said, "I was reading Stephen King."

"Figures," I said.

"Your wishes."

"I would like my first wish to be gifted to a committee of people who have the knowledge and the authority to end world hunger."

"Granted," the genie said.

"Second," I said, "I gift my second wish to a group of people who have the education, experience, authority, and will to figure out global health care, so that any person anywhere in the world can have access to free and qualitative medical treatment and services."

"Granted," the genie said. "Now number three and I'll get back to my novel. You are an incredible bore."

"Noted," I said. "I don't want to gift this third wish. I want to use my last wish."

A long Cheshire-cat smile swept across the genie's face. "By all means," he said.

I could sense his evil intent.

"I wish for your freedom," I said.

"My freedom?" The genie asked.

"Yes," I said. "I wish for you to be free from your bottle, free from granting wishes, free from whomever put you in that bottle in the first place, free from evil intent, free to live, to love, to eat ice cream, to play with puppies, to enjoy the beach, to listen to the breaking waves, to smell the salt in the air. I wish for your freedom."

"Granted," the genie said.

The bottle disappeared. The genie stood before me in swimming gear. He reached out his hand for me to shake. "Thanks," he said. "My name is Omar."

I shook his hand. "Hello, Omar. I'm Steve. Why the swimming gear?"

"I've never been in the ocean before."

"It's February," I said.

"No time like the present," Omar said. He turned and ran toward the water.

I took off my jacket and kicked off my shoes and went running after him.

Chapter Eleven

From Compassion to Action

As I've pointed out numerous times in this book, Jesus' compassion led him to action. First, Jesus' heart was moved with compassion. Then, his compassion led to his healing the sick, feeding the hungry, clothing the naked, and releasing the imprisoned.

I pray our hearts will be moved with compassion for those who are poor and needy. What will compassion lead us to do? Here are a few suggested action steps:

1. Pray.

In Mark 11:24, Jesus says, "Therefore I tell you, whatever you ask for in prayer, believe that you have received it, and it will be yours."

When I don't know what else to do, I pray. That's not the only time I pray, but it's when I pray my best prayers.

I don't know what to do with the statistic like the one that states: today over 20,000 children will die of complications that result from poverty. That statistic staggers me. What can I do about it? There is nothing I can do today to save even one of those 20,000 children, because whatever I decide to do today, it's a day too late.

So I pray.

Prayer is always the correct response.

2. LOVE.

In Matthew 22:39, Jesus says, "Love your neighbor as yourself."

In Mark 12:33, Jesus says, "To love your neighbor as yourself is more important than all burnt offerings and sacrifices."

As we read the gospels, we can't escape LOVE.

Jesus LOVED people.

LOVE is always the correct response.

LOVE fueled by compassion can change the world.

3. Study.

Develop a biblical conviction.

Feelings come and go. Convictions stay.

Know what the Bible says about poverty. Read the Bible from cover to cover and underscore every time the topic occurs.

Then go back and study the topic based on the verses you have underscored.

Read good books on the topic. I recommend Craig L. Blomberg's *Neither Poverty nor Riches: A Biblical Theology of Possessions,* published by InterVarsity Press. I also recommend Ronald J. Sider's *Rich Christians in an Age of Hunger: Moving from Affluence to Generosity* from Thomas Nelson.

Mostly I recommend the gospels. Read Jesus. Let his convictions become your convictions.

4. Contribute.

In the Sermon on the Mount, Jesus says:

"Do not store up for yourselves treasures on earth, where moths and vermin destroy, and where thieves break in and steal. But store up for yourselves treasures in heaven, where moths and vermin do not destroy, and where thieves do not break in and steal. For where your treasure is, there your heart will be also."

Where is your treasure?

Sacrifice financially to help the poor.

If you have any "bigger barns," sell them. Give the proceeds of the sale of your surplus to people who have nothing.

5. Volunteer.

Serve others.

When I serve, it helps my heart.

6. Make this a family decision.

Get everyone in the family involved.

A teen worker in New York City recently gave a survey to the teens in his ministry. He gave them a list of ten items that helped them grow spiritually. Then he asked them to rank these ten items in order of importance from one to ten, with one being the most important item that contributed to their spiritual growth.

Number one was camp. I get that. There is something mystical about teen camp.

Sadly, at the bottom of the list the teens put:

Number ten—Bible talks with adults.

Number nine—the personal example of my parents.

Ouch.

Our children need to see our love in action.

One great way for kids to see the love of their parents in action is through service.

7. Be a good steward.

Whatever you enjoy in life is a gift from God.

Manage your own finances well. Be responsible with what you have.

Since God has shared his bounty with you, learn to share with others.

8. Get other disciples involved in your financial life.

Many of our churches offer financial workshops where you can learn to manage your finances as a good steward. Take one of these workshops.

Also have disciples in your life who will challenge you about greed and materialism. Give them a free pass to challenge you every time they see "a hint of greed" in your life. It is interesting that we have chemical recovery groups and purity groups in our churches, but I've never heard of a greed recovery group. As a church, we have fought hard and with reasonable success to build a culture that is open about our chemical or sexual additions, but we do not do nearly as well with money.

Decide that you will be open with a mature disciple about your spending habits.

9. Begin.

How do we respond to the poverty crisis in our world?

It's an enormous topic. It's weighty. It can paralyze us.

So, what do we do?

Let me ask another question. How do you eat an elephant?

The elephant is enormous. It's weighty. It can paralyze us.

So, how do you eat an elephant?

One bite at a time.

No one person alone can solve world hunger. But God

doesn't expect that of us. He expects us to respond to the plight of the poor with a compassionate heart.

So, where do we begin? With one bite.

Do something.

Begin somewhere.

Start now.

Follow Me
GSK

Jesus said:
Follow me; do not turn back.
Follow me; leave the dead to bury the dead.
Follow me, and I will make you fishermen.
Follow me; take up my cross.

Where does he lead? Where is his path?
It leads to the leper—unloved, untouched, alienated.
It leads to the sinner—guilt-ridden, crushed, lost.
It leads to the poor—hungry, naked, sick, hopeless.
It leads to the Christian brother or sister—weak, struggling, faithless.
It leads to the cross.

No wonder I shudder, I hesitate, I draw back.
Who can follow in that path? Who can bear that cross?

"Lo, I am with you always!"
Dear Jesus, help my unbelief.

A Picture of Poverty

I'm sure you've heard the phrase, "A picture is worth a thousand words." Here is a picture of poverty. I snapped it on a street in Abidjan.

The next time you hear someone say, "Poor people are poor because they are lazy," please show them the picture of this poor woman in Abidjan carrying a tarp filled with the equivalent of a pickup load of stuff. Can any of you imagine walking around the streets of your city with this gigantic burden on your head?

Around the world, most poor people are poor because they were born into poverty and have no way to escape its fateful grasp. No matter how hard they work, how industrious they are, or what benevolent gift they receive, they can't escape the claws of poverty.

So the next time you see a picture like the one of this poor woman trying to cross a busy street in Abidjan, instead of thinking something like, "If she would work harder, she could escape her situation," perhaps you ought to think, "If not for the grace of God, there go I."

Don't blame poverty on laziness. It's just not accurate. Here is a blog I posted after traveling through the countryside of Kenya.

Thursday August 10, 2016
Dr. G. Steve Kinnard

Today we traveled back to Nairobi from Eldoret. The drive reminded me of how massive our mission is. We have targeted the large cities in Africa and throughout the world to plant churches. But as we drove by dozens of villages and farms, I saw thousands of people working in the fields and selling produce by the side of the road (and sometimes in the middle of the road). It reminded me that the majority of the world lives outside the large cities. They live in villages and on farms working hard to make their daily bread in order to survive. Most of these villages have no electricity and no running water. They draw their water from a local well and live off the produce of the land to survive. They often eat only one meal a day, beginning the day with tea, milk, or porridge for breakfast, working through lunch, and sitting down at the close of the day to a supper of sweet potatoes and roasted corn or corn flour meal and vegetables.

Some people claim that poverty is caused by laziness. However, from what I've seen of the poor in Kenya (and other impoverished countries that I have visited), the poor are hardworking and industrious. I've seen little children running after cars and trucks hoping to sell a bag full of green apples, orange carrots, yellow corn, ivory sugar cane, red potatoes and radishes, amber honey, green peas and soy beans, and live chickens of various breeds and colors. I've seen women carrying huge stacks of wood on their backs, which were bent over from the weight of the load. I've seen men out in the fields turning over soil with picks and shovels, making rows in the ground by walking behind plows pulled by cows (and by the way, as I'm writing this, we just crossed the equator). I've seen shepherds walking beside their sheep, and herdsmen walking beside their cows. I've seen men making bricks by hand, others making gravel by crushing rocks with short-handled sledge hammers. These people work hard. And they work hard from sunrise to sunset. Those who sell produce by the roadside earn perhaps 10 to 12 dollars a day (on a good day). Many people live on much, much less. The average person who works on a farm earns 3 to 5 dollars a day. The prayer "Give us this day our daily bread" really means something to the poor in Kenya.

We need to be careful when we make sweeping generalizations about the poor like "the poor are poor because they are lazy." God says in the Proverbs, "Those who mock the poor show contempt for their Maker." Jesus said in reference to helping the poor, "Inasmuch as you did it to one of the least of these My brethren, you did it to Me." Perhaps the inverse of that would also be true, when we make sweeping, derogatory generalizations about the poor, like "the poor are lazy," perhaps we are also making those statements against Jesus, who though "he was rich became poor."

At the prayers before meals in Kenya, it is a practice of the disciples to pray for those who don't have work and don't have food. I urge those of us who live in the First World to adopt this practice. Thus, before we enjoy our meals together, let's take a moment to ask the God of all compassion to throw his arm of protection around those who are hungry and poor, those who are sick who cannot find or afford medical care, those who have been dispossessed of land and property, and those who work long, hard days in hope of a little daily bread.

When you pray for Africa, please remember to pray for the poor of Africa. As you have opportunity, help those who are less fortunate, remembering the words of Jesus, "Inasmuch as you did it to one of the least of these My brethren, you did it to Me." As you look into the eyes of the poor, if you look closely and if you look carefully, you can see the eyes of Jesus.

Conclusion

WWJD?

When I was a young boy (probably around twelve), my mom gave me a book and asked me to read it. It was a short paperback novel. I loved reading, and I loved making Mom happy, so I read the book. Charles Sheldon authored the book and entitled it *In His Steps*. It was first published in 1896. (Some might think I was twelve in 1896, but that's not true.)

The book has haunted me all my life. It tells the story of a preacher who was working on a sermon when he heard a knock on his door. The preacher answered the knock and found a homeless man on his doorstep asking for work. The preacher closed the door on the man and went back into his study to finish his sermon.

The next morning, just as the preacher had finished delivering his Sunday sermon—SPOILER ALERT—the same homeless man walked down the center aisle of the church and stood before the preacher. He turned to face the people in the pews and told about how he wasn't looking for a handout; he was looking for work. Then he died in front of the preacher and the congregation.

The minister felt horribly guilty for the man's death.

The next Sunday, he proposed that each member of the congregation ask a simple question before they made any decision in their life.

The question: What would Jesus do?

That's right: WWJD? Maybe you didn't know that this question was first published in the late nineteenth century.

The question changed the trajectory of the congregation. People began to care about the hurt of others in their community. It revolutionized the ministry of this preacher; his ministry became a ministry of compassion.

I don't know why my mother asked me to read this book at such an early age. She wasn't an advocate of the "social gospel." I don't remember her being active in our community helping people who were down and out. But there was something there. There was a softness to those who had less than we did (and we didn't have much).

The novel slept in my heart throughout my middle school, high school, and college years. Then, in seminary, the book awoke. It caused a deep disturbance in my heart. It led me to read the books of Shailer Matthews, Charles Kingsley, and Walter Rauschenbusch. I found a few slim volumes by Mother Teresa of Calcutta and read those. I found the works of Michael Quiost and the magazine *Sojourners*. An autobiography of Will Campbell shook my world. It seems that everything I read had to do with Jesus and the poor.

I now enter my sixth decade on the earth. Why has it taken me six decades to get to the point that I'm ready to write on Jesus and the poor?

Guilt. Shame. Feelings of being inadequate for the task.

When I was a boy of twelve, I wanted to live in a third-world country and help the poor. During my seminary years, I decided that that country would be India and the city would be Calcutta. Those dreams never materialized.

I live in Fair Lawn, New Jersey, of all places. When I drive, I can occasionally glimpse the skyline of New York City. That's the city of Walter Rauschenbusch. But I'm no Rauschenbusch. No Mother Teresa. No Gandhi. I live too comfortably to write about poverty.

So as I write, I feel guilt. And shame. I feel inadequate to write on this topic.

I wish we had moved to the Third World right out of college. I wish we had moved to Calcutta during our early years in the International Church of Christ instead of staying in New York.

I wish I had not purchased and hoarded as much stuff as I

have over the years. I have regrets. I have so many regrets, too many regrets.

However, I can't live my life paralyzed by regrets. I have to press through my guilt, shame, and inadequacies, and write what is right and biblical and true.

I have to ask myself WWJD?

He would speak the truth in love.

And that's what I've attempted to do in this book.

Please understand that my target audience for writing this book was one person—

Me.

I'm the preacher in Charles Sheldon's book. I'm the preacher who sent the homeless, hungry, unemployed person at my front door away without a meal. I'm that guy.

So I ask you, Dr. G. Steve Kinnard,

WWJD?

THE BEGINNING

Appendix I

Why Help the Poor? A Quiet Time Series

[I wrote these short studies years ago for HOPE *worldwide*. You might have seen them before. I added a couple at the end. I pray you find them useful.]

To accomplish anything in life, we need proper motivation. An important ingredient in proper motivation is that we must understand why we do what we do.

This series of quiet time studies will help us understand why we need to help the poor and why we should have a heart for the poor.

※※※※※※

Day One:
Why Help the Poor? Because God Has a Heart for the Poor.

I know that the LORD secures justice for the poor
and upholds the cause of the needy.

Psalm 140:12

For You (the Lord) have been a defense for the helpless,
A defense for the needy in his distress.

Isaiah 25:4 NASB

He (the Lord) raises the poor from the dust
and lifts the needy from the ash heap.

I Samuel 2:8

Based on what you read in these verses, answer these questions:

- What do you learn about God's heart for the poor?
- List specific ways that God helps the poor.
- If you were poor, how would you be comforted knowing that the Lord is your defense?
- What do these verses teach you about how you should respond to the needs of the poor?
- What are some practical ways that you can work alongside God to "maintain the cause of the afflicted?"

God defends the cause of the poor, the needy, and the afflicted. God has a heart for the poor. When we help the poor, we stand alongside God to defend those who can't help themselves. This is a noble call.

O God, you provided for the poor. Psalm 68:10

Challenge: Before you go out and do something for the poor, begin by checking your motivation. Pray for God to work on you heart. Pray to God and ask him to give you his heart in connection with helping the poor.

✠✠✠✠✠✠

Day Two: Why Help the Poor? Because God Hears the Cries of the Poor.

The poor and needy search for water,
  but there is none;
  their tongues are parched with thirst.
But I the LORD will answer them;
  I, the God of Israel, will not forsake them.

Isaiah 41:17

They (the evildoers) caused the cry of the poor to come
before him (God),
> so that he heard the cry of the needy.

> Job 34:28

- What characteristic or characteristics of God do you see
  demonstrated in these verses?

- If God hears the cries of the poor, then shouldn't we be
  attentive to their cries?

- How can we hear the cry of the poor in our society?

- What are the greatest needs of the people around you?
  Do you hear the cries of those who are poor and hurting
  near you? How can you respond to the tears of the poor?

God hears the cries of the poor, the thirsty, and the hungry.
Do we hear their cries? Today, many people stay insulated from
the cries of the poor. Sometimes this is by choice. Other times it is
because life is so frantic that we don't take time to hear the cry of
the poor. It's like we live in a soundproof booth, shielded from the
hurts and needs of the world around us.

Do we hear the cry of the poor? When you see an appeal
to feed the hungry on television, what is your reaction? Do you
quickly turn the channel? I know I have. It is easy to grow deaf and
callous to the needs of the poor. But God isn't deaf or callous to
their cries. He is attentive. God has a heart for the poor.

My whole being will exclaim,
> "Who is like you, O LORD?
You rescue the poor from those too strong for them,
> the poor and needy from those who rob them."

> Psalm 35:10

I know that the LORD secures justice for the poor
> and upholds the cause of the needy.

> Psalm 140:12

Challenge: Go to the HOPE *worldwide* website and look at the faces of the poor. Imagine that you are hearing their cries. Put yourself in their place. Now pray to God and ask him to help you hear the cry of the poor in the same way that he hears their cries.

Look for the cries of the poor in your community. Find ways to help the poor within your local setting.

✗✗✗✗✗✗

Day Three:
Why Help the Poor? Because Jesus Did.

To this you were called, because Christ suffered for you, leaving you an example, that you should follow in his steps.

I Peter 2:21

Why help the poor? If I were to give only one answer to this question, it would be this—because Jesus did. Jesus had a heart for the poor. He touched lepers. He gave sight to the blind. He caused the lame to walk. He fed the hungry. He preached good news to the poor. He had compassion on people who were hurting, helpless, hapless, and hopeless. Jesus had a heart for the poor.

Matthew 4:23–24 reads:

Jesus went throughout Galilee, teaching in their synagogues, preaching the good news of the kingdom, and healing every disease and sickness among the people. News about him spread all over Syria, and people brought to him all who were ill with various diseases, those suffering severe pain, the demon-possessed, those having seizures, and the paralyzed; and he healed them.

Take a look at the ministry of Jesus:

- Verse 23 models the ministry of Jesus. What three actions are modeled in his ministry? Identify three participles (verbs ending in "ing") in verse 23.

- Does your ministry contain these three characteristics of the ministry of Jesus (teaching, preaching, and healing)? If yes, then how? If no, how can you develop those characteristics in your ministry?

- Many people were brought to Jesus. Describe some of these people.

- When these people were brought to Jesus, what did he do for them?

The ministry of Jesus can be summarized in three words: teaching, preaching, healing. We teach when we open the Bible and share the meaning of Scripture with people. We preach when we share the good news of the gospel with people. We heal when we help people overcome obstacles in their lives that keep them from living a qualitatively good life. (For example, I see our chemical recovery ministry as a healing ministry.)

Jesus healed people of various diseases. It is within our power to help God heal people with disease today. In the next 5 minutes, 19 people will die of disease due to poor sanitation, 8 people will die from malaria, 3 will die from AIDS and 8 more will contract the HIV virus, 7 will be diagnosed with leprosy, 4 will die from measles, 8 will die from chicken pox, and 3 will die from heartworms. All of these are curable or treatable diseases. God has given us the resources to help heal disease across the world today.

Challenge: Think of one way that you can qualitatively help a person change their life. Now reach out and work to find such a person and help them.

�҂ �҂ ✻ ✻ ✻ ✻

Day Four:
Why Help the Poor? Because the Early Church Did.

Around AD 49, leaders of the church in Jerusalem met with Paul and Barnabas to discuss their mission to the Gentiles. This is often referred to as the Jerusalem Council. The Jerusalem Council decided that Gentiles could become Christians without following Jewish ceremonial laws. The Council sent Paul and Barnabas back to the Gentiles to continue their mission.

Paul summarized this event in Galatians 2:9–10 by writing:

> James, Peter and John, those reputed to be pillars, gave me and Barnabas the right hand of fellowship when they recognized the grace given to me. They agreed that we should go to the Gentiles, and they to the Jews. All they asked was that we should continue to remember the poor, the very thing I was eager to do.

When Paul and Barnabas left Jerusalem, the Council could have asked anything of them. They could have asked for monthly reports. They could have asked for revenue to be sent back to Jerusalem. The Council asked them to remember the poor (something that Paul was eager to do). Notice that mission work and service to the poor are complementary ministries. Paul was a missionary who was eager to remember the poor.

- What is the one thing the Jerusalem Council asked that Paul and Barnabas do?
- How did Paul feel about this request?
- Are you eager to remember the poor? Is your ministry group eager to remember the poor?
- How would you define pure and faultless religion?

I might have tricked you with that last question. The definition isn't found in Galatians 2. Pure and faultless religion is defined by James (yes, the same James of the Jerusalem Council). James 1:27 states, "Religion that God our Father accepts as pure and faultless is this: to look after orphans and widows in their distress and to keep oneself from being polluted by the world." James had the poor on his heart.

Church historians record that the early church was known for its compassion. In the Greco-Roman world, when someone didn't want their child, they practiced infanticide. The adult usually placed the child outside the city limits at night exposing the child to the elements. The early church was known for going out at night in search of babies who had been left to die. The disciples would take these babies into their homes, care for them, and raise them as their own. This is one way the early church practiced pure and faultless religion.

Challenge: Is there a widow or widower who lives close to you? Do something nice for this person today.

Day Five:
Why Help the Poor? Because When We Love Others, We Are Good Neighbors.

I'm sure we have all heard the adage, "People don't care how much you know until you show them how much you care."

- How does this statement apply to the Jesus' healing ministry?
- Read Luke 10:25–37, the story of the Good Samaritan.

- Take a moment to picture the victim in this story. How did he look? Try to see his wounds. What might he have said to people as they walked by?

- What are some excuses the priest and Levite might have given for not stopping to help the man in need?

- What are some excuses the Samaritan could have given for not helping?

- Name specific ways that the Samaritan helped the victim.

- Answer Jesus' question in verse 36: "Which of these three do you think was a neighbor to the man who fell into the hands of robbers?"

- What is the last exhortation that Jesus gives to the expert of the law in verse 37? How does this exhortation apply to you?

I read a story of a boy living on the streets in one of our big cities in the northeastern United States during the winter. The boy was standing near a heat exhaust vent to warm himself. The owner of a clothing store saw the boy and thought about offering him some help. Before he made the offer, a customer interrupted his thoughts by asking for assistance, and the storeowner forgot about the boy. He left the boy in the cold.

Later, the man saw the boy in his store. He was with a woman who had invited the boy into the store to purchase him clothes. She was buying the boy new shoes, new gloves, and a new coat.

The storeowner overheard the boy ask the woman, "Are you God's wife?"

The woman answered, "No, I'm just one of his children."

The boy said, "Well, I knew you were related to him somehow."

- Who was a neighbor to the little boy?

Challenge: Think of the needs of the poor in your town or community. How can you be a Good Samaritan to someone today? Now "go and do likewise."

✵ ✵ ✵ ✵ ✵ ✵

**Day Six:
Why Help the Poor? Because When You Help the Poor, You Help Yourself.**

It is a sin to despise one's neighbor,
but blessed is the one who is kind to the needy.

Proverbs 14:21

The generous will themselves be blessed (happy),
for they share their food with the poor.

Proverbs 22:9

Give generously to [the needy among you] and do so without a grudging heart; then because of this the LORD your God will bless you in all your work and in everything you put your hand to.

Deuteronomy 15:10

Whoever is kind to the poor lends to the LORD,
and he will reward them for what they have done.

Proverbs 19:17

In everything I (Paul) did, I showed you that by this kind of hard work we must help the weak, remembering the words the Lord Jesus himself said: "It is more blessed to give than to receive."

Acts 20:35

- What happens to the person who gives generously to the poor?

- Proverbs 19:17 states, "Whoever is kind to the poor lends to the Lord." Imagine in your mind's eye God smiling at you when you are gracious to the poor. Carry that image with you throughout the day.

- Think of a time when you have given to the poor. How have you been blessed because of that act?

Every time I have taken time to give to the poor, it has helped my own heart more than I have helped the needy. Paul quotes a saying of Jesus that is not found in the gospels, "It is more blessed to give than to receive." The word "blessed" can also mean "happy." Jesus states a truth here, "We are happier when we give than when we receive." I feel happy when I help the poor. Whether I'm washing dishes at a soup kitchen, teaching martial arts at a HOPE *worldwide* school, or delivering food to seniors, I come back from those activities feeling like I've done something that has brought glory to God. The more I give, the happier I am. Why? Because when we give, God blesses our hearts.

Challenge: Perform one "random act of kindness" to someone today. Be a giver. When you give, pay attention to the joy the act of giving brings to your life.

Day Seven:
Why Help the Poor? Because When We Help the Poor, We See That Possessions Are Not Important.

Whenever I am with the poor, I am reminded of how much my life is cluttered with stuff. The poor live with so little. They teach me that life can be lived without rooms full of stuff.

> But among you there must not be even a hint of sexual immorality, or of any kind of impurity, or of greed, because these are improper for God's holy people.
>
> Ephesians 5:3

- Paul names three specific vices in this passage that we must not allow even a hint of into our lives. Name them.

- Why must we be vigilant against these three vices?

- In what ways are you tempted with greed?

- How do you act on that temptation?

- How do you fight against that temptation?

Read the parable of Jesus in Luke 12:6–21.

- What are ways that you store up things for yourself?
- How can you become rich toward God?

In our culture, we don't necessarily buy bigger barns; we just rent a storage space for all our excess stuff. We fill our attics and garages. So we do build bigger barns—today they are called self-storage units.

Most of the world could live and would love to live on what we throw away—and many would love to have a living space the size of a storage unit to call their own. We need to take a good look at our lifestyles. Where does all our stuff get us? Do things satisfy? We want more. The bills pile up. The stuff accumulates, so we get more space. Indirectly, we teach our children that things will make us happy. But we don't find true happiness in things. Isn't it time for us to simplify our lives? Wouldn't it be more satisfying to live on less so that others might simply live?

Challenge: Remove clutter from your life. Find something that you haven't used in years and give it to someone who can use it.

✲✲✲✲✲✲

Day Eight:
Why Help the Poor? Because If You Don't, Then Beware!

When you drive, you pay attention to warning signs. Falling Rock! Dangerous Turn! Construction Ahead! Slippery Conditions!

The Bible gives warning signs. The Word gives many stern warnings for people who callously overlook the needs of the poor and needy, such as:

> Whoever shuts their ears to the cry of the poor
> will also cry out and not be answered.
>
> Proverbs 21:13

> Those who give to the poor will lack nothing,
> but those who close their eyes to them receive many curses.
>
> Proverbs 28:27

- What happens to the person who shuts their ear to the cry of the poor?
- What happens to the person who closes their eyes to the poor?

Let these words from the Proverbs ring in your ears. There are repercussions that come from allowing your heart to become callous to the cry of the poor. God hears their cry; we need to stay attuned to it as well.

The Bible also issues warnings to those who are rich in this world. With riches comes responsibility.

Read the words of Jesus in Luke 6:20–25.

- List the blessings of the poor, the hungry, the grieving, and the hated.

- List the woes pronounced against the rich, the well fed, and those who laugh now.

- Why did Jesus paint such a stark contrast between the poor and rich?

Allow me to give you one last warning. This one is stated in all three of the synoptic gospels (Matthew, Mark, and Luke). Jesus says, "Again I tell you, it is easier for a camel to go through the eye of a needle than for someone who is rich to enter the kingdom of God" (Matthew 19:24).

- Why would Jesus make this statement?

Jesus issued some strong warnings against the rich. He followed the tradition of the prophets of Israel in condemning people who covetously clung to their wealth while others around them barely survived. God expects those of us who are rich to have compassionate hearts toward the poor.

Challenge: Pray. Pray for the needs of the poor around the world. Pray for the needs of the poor within your local community. I often don't know what to do with the overwhelming feeling that no matter how much I do for the poor it seems like it is too little or too inconsequential. But there is always one response that is appropriate—prayer.

�֎ ✖ ✖ ✖ ✖ ✖

Day Nine:
Why Help the Poor? Because the Poor Desperately Need Our Help.

The poor and needy search for water,
>   but there is none;
>   their tongues are parched with thirst.
But I the LORD will answer them;
>   "I, the God of Israel, will not forsake them.
I will make rivers flow on barren heights,
>   and springs within the valleys.
I will turn the desert into pools of water,
>   and the parched ground into springs.
I will put in the desert
>   the cedar and the acacia, the myrtle and the olive.
I will set junipers in the wasteland,
>   the fir and the cypress together,
so that people may see and know,
>   may consider and understand,
that the hand of the LORD has done this,
>   that the Holy One of Israel has created it."

Isaiah 41:17–20

The poor are desperate. God reacts to their desperation. How will we respond to their plight?

Today over a billion people live and die in abject poverty. These one billion people live on a little less than a dollar a day. More than two billion others live on less than two dollars a day. One cup of Starbucks coffee could pay the daily salaries of four people living in the Third World.

In the United States, most of our dogs and cats eat more food and receive better medical care than most of the people in the Third World. The typical American spends more on his dog or cat than the average person living in the Third World will see in his lifetime.

Today, around 20,000 children will die from conditions that result from poverty.

- If 20,000 children died in the United States or anywhere else in the First World today, what would be the response of global leaders?
- Imagine what the outcry would be if tomorrow the newspaper headlines read, "Yesterday across the United States 20,000 children died." What would be the response of people across the United States?
- What would happen if a first-world country had to plan for 20,000 burials for children within its borders? Then, the next day, another 20,000 funerals. What would the response be?

Challenge: Spend some time today reading about the plight of the poor in various parts of the world. Read some articles that will help you understand the daily life of the poor. Put yourself in the shoes of a poor person in Africa or Southeast Asia. Feel that person's desperation. Then share what you learned with another person.

Day Ten: Warning: Beware of Riches

The Surgeon General of the United States has posted a warning on the packages of cigarettes that smoking is hazardous to your health. If you travel in parts of Europe, pictures of charred, blackened lungs often accompany these warnings against smoking. It's amazing to me that after seeing these pictures, people still choose to purchase cigarettes. But that's the price of addiction.

What if warnings came with the accumulation of riches? Given the number of times the Bible warns us of the harmful impact of riches on our spiritual lives, it seems appropriate.

Consider these verses:

> Do not wear yourself out to get rich;
> do not trust your own cleverness.
> Cast but a glance at riches, and they are gone,
> for they will surely sprout wings
> and fly off to the sky like an eagle.
>
> Proverbs 23:4–5

> Keep falsehood and lies far from me;
> give me neither poverty nor riches,
> but give me only my daily bread.
> Otherwise, I may have too much and disown you
> and say, "Who is the LORD?"
> Or I may become poor and steal,
> and so dishonor the name of my God.
>
> Proverbs 30:8–9

> Whoever loves money never has enough;
> whoever loves wealth is never satisfied with their income.
> This too is meaningless.
> As goods increase,
> so do those who consume them.
> And what benefit are they to the owners
> except to feast their eyes on them?
> The sleep of a laborer is sweet,
> whether they eat little or much,
> but as for the rich, their abundance
> permits them no sleep.
> I have seen a grievous evil under the sun:
> wealth hoarded to the harm of its owners,
> or wealth lost through some misfortune,
> so that when they have children
> there is nothing left for them to inherit.

Everyone comes naked from their mother's womb,
    and as everyone comes, so they depart.
They take nothing from their toil
    that they can carry in their hands.

Ecclesiastes 5:10–15

"It is easier for a camel to go through the eye of a needle than for someone who is rich to enter the kingdom of God."

Mark 10:25

"But woe to you who are rich,
    for you have already received your comfort."

Luke 6:24

"But Abraham replied, 'Son, remember that in your lifetime you received your good things, while Lazarus received bad things, but now he is comforted here and you are in agony.'"

Luke 16:25

Those who want to get rich fall into temptation and a trap and into many foolish and harmful desires that plunge people into ruin and destruction. For the love of money is a root of all kinds of evil. Some people, eager for money, have wandered from the faith and pierced themselves with many griefs.

1 Timothy 6:9–10

- What do you think of these verses?
- How do they serve as a warning against the accumulation of wealth?
- Is there a hint of greed in your life?

Challenge: Find something in your life that you can give up or sell and contribute the finances from that sacrifice to the poor.

Appendix II

50 Ways to Help the Poor

1. Donate food to your church food pantry, or if they don't have one, donate to your local food pantry.
2. Choose a day to serve at a local food pantry. Check their website; most contain requirements for service.
3. Respect people who are poor or homeless. Give them the same courtesy and goodwill that you would accord your friends, your family, or your employer. Treat them as you would wish to be treated if you needed assistance.
4. Respond with kindness to all those in need. We can make quite a difference in the lives of people who are destitute when we love them rather than ignore or dismiss them. Try a kind word and a smile. Don't assume they are in this predicament because of bad choices.
5. Get freezer-size zipper-lock plastic bags and create "care packages" with bottled water or an electrolyte drink, a nutritious snack, and a church invite. Keep four or five in your car and distribute them as the opportunity arises.
6. Purchase $5 gift certificates from various fast food restaurants to give away as needed.
7. Volunteer at a nursing or senior adult center. Mother's or Father's Day are great days to visit. Ask the director of the facility which patients most need encouragement or get few visits from relatives.
8. Contact your State's Department of Social Services and get certified to be a foster parent. The majority of states are greatly in need of foster parents.
9. Adopt a child. In many states, children can be adopted at no cost through the Department of Social Services. Adopting

children in need helps break the cycle of poverty.

10. Donate money to help families who are in the process of adopting.

11. Downgrade your cell phone or cable plan and donate the money to HOPE *worldwide* or some favorite charity that helps the poor.

12. Drop off toys or handheld video games at your local children's hospital (most hospitals' websites will have a list of needed items).

13. Carefully go through your closet and donate all clothes and shoes that you no longer use. Perhaps even downsize your wardrobe and donate the excess to Goodwill or the Salvation Army.

14. Downsize your electronics collection (televisions, iPads, Kindles, etc.) and give to church friends in need or to the poor in your community.

15. If you have spare or guest bedrooms, open your home to host people at no cost who are receiving medical treatment or have other needs.

16. Sponsor a child through Compassion International or Food for the Hungry.

17. Sign up to coach a youth sport in a poor community in your city. Use the opportunity to tell kids they're smart, needed, and important.

18. Donate time and money for Meals on Wheels or other organizations that serve the elderly who are homebound or disabled.

19. Sign up to drive cancer patients or others in need of medical service to their appointments.

20. Start a group in your church that is dedicated to home repairs and housework to help single moms and other needy individuals.

21. Find a widow or widower in your neighborhood and invite them to your home for a meal.

22. Research and compile a list of soup kitchens, homeless shelters, and free medical clinics to print out and give out to the homeless and needy.

23. Find out the items most needed by your local homeless shelter (e.g., towels, blankets, socks) and donate them.

24. Mentor disciples who are unemployed or underemployed on how to improve their job skills or how to work harder to improve their value to employers.

25. For those who are perpetually unemployed, help them to develop skills that are required by the marketplace. Spend some weekly time helping them research jobs that may be suitable to their skills.

26. Build a relationship with someone who is indigent. Offer to be their friend and personal coach, monitoring their weekly progress until they become independent and productive.

27. Set up a donation drop box and invite the community to donate items that will help the needy.

28. Buy an MP3 player (you can find many inexpensive models now) and fill it with uplifting songs, some sermons, and an audible version of the New Testament. Give it to a homeless or needy person.

29. Instead of having a garage sale, take all those items and donate them to an organization that helps the poor.

30. Volunteer your professional services. You can help people who are homeless with your job talent and skills. Doctors, psychiatrists, counselors, and dentists can treat the homeless in free medical clinics. Lawyers can help with legal concerns.

31. Volunteer for follow-up programs. Some people who are indigent need help and training with fundamental tasks such as paying bills, balancing a household budget, or cleaning.

Follow-up programs to give further advice, counseling, and training are extremely important to help the poor become independent and successful.

32. Tutor homeless children. A tutor can make all the difference. Just having extra attention can motivate a child to do their best. Many programs exist in shelters, transitional housing programs, and schools that need interested volunteers. Begin your own tutor volunteer corps at your church.

33. Help tutor the poor, or recent immigrants, especially teaching them English. Education is one of the greatest tools in moving someone toward self-sufficiency.

34. Volunteer at shelters that serve battered women. Most women who are battered are involved in abusive relationships. Lacking resources and afraid of being found by their abusers, many have no recourse other than a shelter or life on the streets. These shelters are especially in need of donations. Call to see how you can help.

35. Educate your children and get them involved. Volunteer as a family at a shelter or housing program. Suggest that your children sort through their toys, books, and clothes and donate some to organizations that help the poor and needy.

36. Donate a weekend to serve with Habitat for Humanity. This housing ministry builds homes for families who are in great need or who are in danger of becoming homeless.

37. Donate blood in your community. Donate plasma and give the funds to indigent medical care.

38. Fast at least one day a week on behalf of the poor and donate the money saved each month to a worthy cause.

39. Plan a mission trip to serve the needy in a third-world country (check HOPE *worldwide* for current and future opportunities).

40. Sign up to be an organ donor. It's a great way to serve those who are in medical crisis, and you won't need that body where

you are going anyway!

41. Do your best to always donate your time, energy, and money when you congregation is doing an activity to raise funds to help the poor. The more people are involved, the more good work can be done for the cause of Christ and the needs of the poor.

42. Take the time and initiative to educate other disciples, families, and friends about the needs of the poor. More would help, if they only knew.

43. Provide free babysitting for a needy single mom.

44. Write your local civic leaders, politicians, and others of influence to advocate for government programs that will help meet the needs of the poor.

45. Education is one of the most important tools to eradicate poverty. Donate money to schools that specialize in teaching the poor and needy.

46. Volunteer your time at local hospitals that provide indigent care. Volunteer needs are usually available on their websites.

47. Find an elderly person or couple in your area and volunteer to mow their yard, clean their home, or run errands for them.

48. Be a mentor to kids in need. Big Brothers, Big Sisters, and similar organizations are great ways to meet the needs of kids.

49. Help sponsor a needy kid for a summer church camp or program.

50. Donate money to organizations that provide source funding for sustainable small business creation in third-world countries.

Appendix III

Facts on Global Poverty and Hunger

Around the world, 767 million people live in extreme poverty with less than $1.90 per person per day, an amount on which it is impossible to support a healthy living in any part of the world.

One in three children in low- and middle-income countries suffers from chronic undernutrition. Without a sustainable source of income at a sufficient level, young children and their families do not have access to nutritious food, clean water, or health care. And the deadly effects of malnutrition cannot be underestimated: 45% of all child deaths worldwide are from causes related to malnutrition; that's 3.1 million children.

GLOBAL POVERTY FACTS

Here are some statistics that show the scale of poverty and its devastating effects.

- 767 million people, or 10.7 percent of the world population, live in extreme poverty, with less than $1.90 per day.

- 2.1 billion people live on less than $3.10 per day.

- 328 million children are living in extreme poverty.

- At least 17 million children around the world suffer from severe acute undernutrition. Severe acute malnutrition is the direct cause of death for 1 million children every year.

- Every single day, 1000 children under 5 die from illnesses like diarrhea, dysentery, and cholera caused by contaminated water and inadequate sanitation.

Stats 1-3: World Bank, 4-5: Unicef

WHERE IS EXTREME POVERTY?

Africa is the continent with the largest number of people living in extreme poverty. Here is a breakdown of where people living with less than $2.00 per day are located:

- 383 Million in Africa (Nigeria 86M, Congo 56M, Tanzania 22M)

- 327 Million in Asia (India 218M, China, 25M, Indonesia 24M)

- 19 Million in South America (Brazil 10M, Colombia 3M)

- 13 Million in North America (Haiti 5.5M, Mexico 3.5M)

- 2.5 Million in Oceania

- 0.7 in Europe

CHILDREN LIVING IN EXTREME POVERTY

It is estimated that 104 million children under age 5 are living in extreme poverty, while that number extends to 328 million for children under 18 (World Bank, 2016).

Children suffer the most when living in poverty. Their young, developing bodies are less resilient to the effects of living without clean water, food, or health care. As a result, many children living in poverty suffer malnutrition and disease. If left untreated—which is common due to limited access to health care—they cannot survive. It is estimated that only 10% of children suffering from severe acute malnutrition receive proper treatment.[46]

---

[46] Information courtesy of www.actionagainsthunger.org

Bibliography

Arthur, Douglas and Douglas Jacoby, *I Was Hungry,* Second Edition. London: Central London Church of Christ, 1987.

Beckmann, David and Arthur Simon. *Grace at the Table: Ending Hunger in God's World.* Downers Grove, IL: InterVarsity Press, 1999.

Blomberg, Craig L. *Neither Poverty nor Riches: A Biblical Theology of Possessions.* Downers Grove, IL: InterVarsity Press, 1999.

Bonhoeffer, Dietrich. *The Cost of Discipleship.* New York: Macmillan, 1966.

Boucher, Douglas H., ed. *Paradox of Plenty: Hunger in a Bountiful World.* Food First, Oakland. 1999.

de Santa Ana, J. *Good News to the Poor: The Challenge of the Poor in the History of the Church.* Geneva: WCC, 1977.

Dunson, Donald H. *No Room at the Table: Earth's Most Vulnerable Children.* Maryknoll, NY: Orbis, 2003.

Foster, Richard J. *Celebration of Discipline.* Second Edition. San Francisco: Harper Collins, 1988.

_____. *Freedom of Simplicity.* San Francisco: Harper & Row, 1981.

_____. *Money, Sex & Power.* San Francisco: Harper & Row, 1985.

McGovern, George S. *The Third Freedom: Ending Hunger in Our Time.* New York: Simon and Schuster, 2001.

McGovern, George, and Bob Dole and Donald E. Messer. *Ending Hunger Now.* Minneapolis, MN: Augsburg Fortress, 2005.

Mealand, D. L. *Poverty and Expectation in the Gospels,* London: SPCK, 1980.

Pilgrim, W. E. *Good News to the Poor. Wealth and Poverty in Luke–Acts.* Minneapolis, MN: Augsburg Fortress, 1981.

Russell, Sharman Apt. *Hunger: An Unnatural History.* New York: Basic Books, 2006.

Seccombe, D. P. *Possessions and the Poor in Luke–Acts.* In SNTU 6. Linz, Austria: n.p., 1982.

Sider, Ronald J. *Rich Christians in an Age of Hunger: Moving from Affluence to Generosity.* Nashville, TN: Thomas Nelson, 2005.

Themelios: Volume 12, No. 3, April 1987. United Kingdom: The Gospel Coalition, 1987.

Woolman, John. *The Journal of John Woolman.* Secaucus, NJ: Citadel Press, 1972.

Your Kingdom Come: Mission Perspectives. Report on the World Conference on Mission and Evangelism. Melbourne, 1980/Geneva, 1980.

Books by G. Steve Kinnard

Books by G. Steve Kinnard

SPIRITUAL PERSONAL DEVELOPMENT
FOR THE EVERYDAY CHRISTIAN

Like A Tree
Planted by
Streams of Water

DR. G. STEVE KINNARD

G. STEVE KINNARD

An Introduction
and Topical Index to
the Book of Proverbs

THE
CALL
OF THE
WISE

A Practical Exposition

THE GOSPEL OF
MATTHEW

The Crowning
of the King

G. Steve Kinnard

Books by G. Steve Kinnard

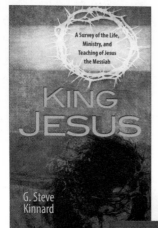

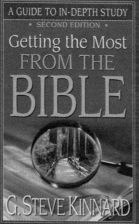

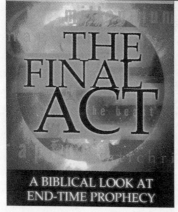

All of G. Steve Kinnard's books are available at

www.ipibooks.com

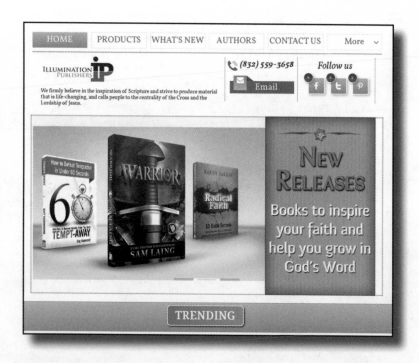